The RFU
Rugby Union
Referee's Manual

written by Richard Greensted

London

First published 1997 by
A & C Black (Publishers) Ltd
35 Bedford Row, London WC1R 4JH

ISBN 0 7136 4614 4

Acknowledgments
Photographs on the front cover and pages iii, vi, 6, 56, 103,
104 and 116 courtesy of Colorsport.
Photograph on page 35 courtesy of Abbey Studios, Wolverhampton.
All others photographs courtesy of the Rugby Football Union.

This book has been typeset in Trump Mediaeval 11/12pt
Printed and bound in Great Britain by
Hillman Printers (Frome) Ltd., Somerset.

• CONTENTS •

CHAPTER 4
Restarts 57

CHAPTER 5
Getting on 85

APPENDIX 1
Referee signals 105

APPENDIX 2
Referee Societies 117

Foreword

The game of rugby has had to contend with many changes in a short space of time. As referees, we have needed to keep pace with these changes. Many training programmes have been introduced to help facilitate the modern game.

As part of this initiative, I am delighted that the RFU has now produced a manual for referees. This manual gives referees an excellent insight into what is expected of them, as well as offering sound practical advice and support on all aspects of refereeing.

At the same time, the manual will assist in accelerating the development of new referees and will also act as very useful reference point for even the most experienced referee.

I'm convinced that regular reading of this manual will enhance the performance of any referee, allowing all participants - referees and players alike - to maximise their enjoyment of this wonderful game.

Ed Morrison
RFU Panel of National Referees
International referee
1995 Rugby World Cup final referee

Author's note

Inevitably, the production of this manual has depended heavily on the wisdom, advice and counsel of many people.

I would especially like to thank Steve Griffiths, National Referee Development Officer of the Rugby Football Union from 1993 to 1997, who gave much guidance and encouragement; Keith Bonser, RFU Divisional Technical Administrator (Midlands), who added valuable commentary on the players' perspective; Jimmy Crowe, a member of the RFU's Laws Advisory Panel, who dealt swiftly and constructively with questions of Law; and Ian Dorrn, a good friend who has always been ready to listen and help.

I also want to thank everyone at the Metropolitan Surrey Society of Rugby Football Referees: without their excellent training, commitment and dedication, I would not have been able to write this book.

Two final points to note.

(1) This manual is based on the Laws for the 1997/8 season.
(2) As we all know, an increasing number of women are becoming referees. For the purposes of style I have used the masculine form throughout the book, but all such references apply equally to women.

Richard Greensted
Richard is an active referee and is General Secretary of the Metropolitan Surrey Society of Rugby Football Referees. He has written two business books and three novels.

CHAPTER 1

Who'd be a referee?

You've just watched a game of rugby. Perhaps it was at your local club; perhaps one of your children was playing at school or in a mini-rugby tournament; or perhaps it was the climax of the Five Nations Championship. But now you're saying to yourself: 'I could do that. I could be a referee, and I could probably do a far better job than the one I've just seen!'

So what do you do next? What sort of person becomes a referee, and what's involved once you get started? This manual aims to tell you what you need to know about refereeing - before, during and after the actual game. By the time you've finished reading this book, you should have a very clear idea of whether you've got what it takes - although nobody really knows that until they've run out on to the pitch with a whistle in their pocket. Existing referees may also learn something useful from this book, as it never does any harm to confirm your understanding of the skills involved.

The scenario above is just one of the motivations for becoming a referee. Rugby is a sport which encourages and welcomes participation at all levels, from playing, refereeing and administration to serving the post-match teas. It's a sport which is still primarily played for fun, in spite of the advent of the open game. On chilly Saturday afternoons friendly games are played the length and breadth of the country, with no rewards available other than the satisfaction of having enjoyed 80 minutes of rugby. For the game to work at this level, there must be an abundant and continuing supply of volunteers - and referees are the most important volunteers of all. Without a referee, you can't have a game.

Typically, rugby referees have been drawn from the pool of ex-players. Players who have reached a certain age, or who have had to retire due to injury, work or family commitments, can still participate as referees, and will be providing a vital service to the game if they do. But it isn't just ex-players with cauliflower ears and broken noses who aspire to refereeing; the motivation to become a rugby referee stems from a number of different sources.

1

Whilst giving something back to the game is clearly a major factor, there are other reasons for taking up the whistle.

- To help to raise the standard of refereeing.
- To contribute to players' enjoyment of the game.
- To keep fit and active.
- To stay in touch with the game.
- Most importantly, to have some fun.

Whatever the motivation, there is a place for you in the game. Referees are not born, they are made. There is no single type of person who is the perfect referee: they come from all walks of life, and they all have their idiosyncrasies and foibles. In fact, refereeing is very much like playing: it doesn't matter where you come from, or who you are, as long as you can perform on the pitch.

The tools of the trade

Some will say that refereeing is an art, some a science - but it is neither. Refereeing is a skill and, like any other skill, it can be taught and learnt. Most referees are only limited by their personal ambitions and aspirations: if they want to get to the top, and they're good enough, they will. But there are characteristics which the referee needs to have if he is to succeed.

Firstly, he needs to have an **empathy** with the game. It is difficult, but not impossible, to referee a rugby match if you don't have some intrinsic understanding of, and feeling for, the game. After all, you are planning to go out there and look after 30 players for 80 minutes: if you don't understand what they're trying to achieve, and you can't differentiate between positive and negative play, you're going to get into trouble. This is why ex-players have a headstart when it comes to refereeing. But knowing the game from the players' perspective isn't enough, and can sometimes put you at a disadvantage: the skill of refereeing is so different, and requires such altered levels of concentration, fitness and positioning, that recently retired players can easily find themselves in a mess early on in their refereeing career. It takes time to adjust to the new demands.

Secondly, the successful referee will be a good **communicator**. Later in this book we will look at the subject of communication in some depth, but it's important to understand that the rugby referee, as distinct from many other sports, talks and signals almost constantly during a game. The players need the referee to tell them what he expects from them, and what he is looking for. In this respect, the referee acts in a preventive capacity, advising players on what course of action to take so that they do not infringe. This is not cheating, and it is not contrary to the spirit or the Laws of the game: referees are positively encouraged to develop these communication skills so that games under their control are well managed and enjoyable for the players.

Thirdly, the referee must be **fit.** Fitness is obviously relative, but you need to be able to keep up with play, to change pace and direction quickly, to recover rapidly, and to have enough in reserve that you can still make good decisions. You should aim to be at least as fit as the players you will referee.

These three elements make up the base requirement for a rugby referee, and they could all be listed under the heading of **management** skills. Managing a game is not simply blowing the whistle when an infringement occurs and keeping the score and time. Game management encompasses empathy, communication, and fitness, as well as knowledge of the Laws. You have to know the Laws: there are 28, some more important than others, but they all need to be learnt and, more critically, understood. What are the motivations for each Law? What are they trying to achieve? How should they be interpreted? Knowing the answers to questions such as these is part of the skill of refereeing.

Help is at hand

So rugby refereeing is a challenge, not a soft option. That challenge can only be met if you are properly prepared and fully confident. Fortunately, there is a huge infrastructure in place to support you, train you, encourage you, and develop you. Referees carry a large burden of responsibility, and they are not expected to shoulder this alone. In fact, the Foreword to the Laws actually states that: *It is the duty of Unions to ensure that the Game at every level is conducted in accordance with disciplined and sporting behaviour. This principle cannot be upheld solely by the referee; its observance also rests on Unions, affiliated bodies and clubs.* The game is on your side from the word 'go'; volunteer to become a referee and you will immediately benefit from the combined support of administrators, players and coaches. The game needs referees, and fully recognises their importance.

Most referees start out with their local Referee Society. They may have done a couple of 'Extra B' XV games at their club to help out but, as likely as not, they will have no real experience of refereeing. Few will ever have seen a Law book, let alone have read it! Referee Societies are locally organised, and are administered by current and former referees. Although these Societies are entirely separate from the game's central and regional administrators, they act in close co-operation with them. The principle of most Societies is that they organise referee resources on behalf of the clubs they serve, for which they are paid a fee by those clubs to cover their costs. Their primary function is to allocate referees to club fixtures; as an additional service, they organise training and development of their member referees, teachers, and club referees. Comprehensive training and development programmes are provided to the Societies by the game's central administrators.

Joining a Society is pretty painless and is usually free. It need not commit you to refereeing: many Societies organise and run open days for potential referees so that they can get a feel of what's involved and the commitment that's required. If you're still keen, you can join and ease your way into refereeing. But, as with everything else in life, if you really want to know what's involved, you've got to do it for yourself. Getting a game and refereeing it, however intimidating that may sound, is the only true way to tell whether it's for you. No-one will be upset if you discover that it isn't - but you're more likely to be pleasantly surprised! There's more about Societies and their work in Chapter 5.

Hopes and dreams

It is easy, and perfectly understandable, to be intimidated by the concept of refereeing. If you come in to the game with little knowledge of the Laws, and even less experience, it can seem like a fairly daunting task. Suddenly you are required to know the Laws intimately - something that is not necessary for players - and you are no longer part of the playing fraternity: you are the classic poacher turned gamekeeper. You may be concerned about how players, coaches and spectators will treat you, and whether you will be blamed for everything that goes wrong on the pitch. But, whilst it's true that you need a thick skin to be a good referee, it's also true that, if you do your job well and are consistent and fair, you will earn the respect of players. Unlike some other sports, there is no 'them and us' mentality in rugby: players and coaches appreciate the contribution of a good referee and will be quite happy to discuss your performance with you in the bar after the game. If you think of yourself as the 31st player on the pitch, it will give you much more confidence about your role as a referee.

You will also find that the same concerns, hopes and fears are shared by all rugby referees, however senior they may be. One of the great things about the game is that you, as a trainee referee, can be sitting in the club changing room with very senior referees with years of experience, and they will gladly share that experience with you. You need only ask: there's no such thing as a stupid question when it comes to refereeing! Every referee started the same way, and they all remember only too well how puzzling it can all be at the beginning.

The other beauty of refereeing is that you can go as far as you want. When you start you may have dreams of ending up as a World Cup Final referee and, if you're good enough, you'll be in contention. But all participants in the game realise that it is not just World Cup referees who are needed: it is equally important to have a dedicated corps of referees who will handle the more junior games, those men and women who will happily turn out each week for friendlies. The game is built on these foundations - and, of course, the top players work their way through the ranks in exactly the same way as referees. At whatever level you choose to participate, you are providing an invaluable service. Even if you can only turn out once a month, that is one more fixture which will benefit from a qualified referee, and 30 more satisfied players. The business of refereeing is both democratic and pragmatic.

The game needs you

Refereeing is rather like golf. When you start, you wonder what all the fuss is about because it seems so easy. But, as you progress, you realise that it is an incredibly challenging exercise, and you can never relax or rest on your laurels. You learn to be more critical of your own performance, and you start to focus on the areas that need your attention rather than the things you know you can do well. It becomes addictive and, in your determination to improve, you set ever higher standards. You never stop learning, and you never stop needing the advice and coaching of others.

With all the changes that have taken place in rugby over the past few years, there is a growing requirement for qualified referees. Sadly, there are still too many fixtures for the Referee Societies to cover, although a lot of work has been done to bring new referees into the sport. The game of rugby is not just what you see on television - the internationals and the national leagues and cups - but the thousands of matches played throughout the country every week. If the game is to improve, many more qualified referees have to be found so that players can perform to their full potential.

So the answer to the title of this chapter - 'Who'd be a referee?' - is simple: people like you. You're reading this, which means that you have some interest in finding out more. Whatever your back-ground, there's probably a place for you in the game, and there are certainly plenty of people who will help you to find it. You only have to ask.

The purpose of this book is to give you some advice on how to become a better referee. By itself, reading the book will not improve your performance, but it will help you to understand what's required. You have to put the theory into practice, and you'll find that it's well worth the effort - refereeing is far more enjoyable if you know what you're doing!

CHAPTER 2

The principles of management

Rugby is a game that encompasses a fascinating mixture of differing skills and demands. It is about power, strength, endurance, agility and speed, qualities which are nowadays required from all players, regardless of their position. The Laws have been adapted to encourage and reward these attributes, and coaches have recognised the need to develop new skills in their players to meet the challenge.

Bearing this in mind, it is perhaps surprising that the entire game can be summed up in a very succinct way in Law 7, Mode of Play. This states that:

A match is started by a kick-off, after which any player who is on-side and provided he does so in accordance with these Laws may at any time:

- *catch or pick up the ball and run with it*
- *pass, throw or knock the ball to another player*
- *kick or otherwise propel the ball*
- *tackle, push or shoulder an opponent holding the ball*
- *fall on the ball*
- *take part in scrummage, ruck, maul or line-out*
- *ground the ball in in-goal.*

That, in short, is the framework for the game of rugby union. The other Laws put flesh on the bones, but Law 7 is the foundation.

It's useful to learn Law 7 in its entirety, because it tells you very precisely how the game is played. If you start off with an understanding of this Law, the others will be much easier to understand and apply.

However, rugby remains a flexible and versatile sport. It can be played in a variety of ways, and no two games will ever be the same. But, for the referee, each game will contain critical phases and elements that must be monitored and managed effectively for both players and spectators to get the maximum enjoyment from the contest.

These phases can be summarised in three categories: **management, continuity, and restarts**. In subsequent chapters we'll look at continuity and restarts, and examine how the referee should manage them. Before that, however, we need to consider the key skills of overall management.

(1) The role of the referee

The Foreword to the Laws states: *The Object of the Game is that two teams of 15, ten or seven players each, observing fair play according to the Laws and a sporting spirit, should by carrying, passing, kicking and grounding the ball score as many points as possible, the team scoring the greater number of points to be the winner of the match. The Laws of the Game ... are complete and contain all that is necessary to enable the game to be played correctly and fairly. It is the duty of the referee to apply fairly the Laws of the Game without any variation or omission.*

Put like that, the role of the referee seems pretty straightforward. In practice, however, things aren't quite that simple. The referee faces a series of challenges and must have the necessary skills to apply fundamental principles to his management of the game. What is the precise role of the referee, and what should the players expect from him?

(1.1) The referee as game manager

No matter what the level, there is one primary objective for the referee: **to manage an environment in which two sides can play and enjoy a game of rugby football within the Laws of the game.**

How do you set about the task of achieving that objective? As the 31st participant in the game, the referee plays a pivotal role - yet no-one goes to a match to watch the referee. In fact, the best compliment that can be paid to a referee is to hear it said: 'What a wonderful game that was!' By association, the referee can't have done a bad job. As a manager, the referee needs to be in control and to exercise his skills without overpowering the action, unobtrusively creating that special environment in which good rugby can be played and enjoyed.

The role of the referee is to create a situation which allows the participants to play to the best of their ability. The referee cannot make people play well, but he can give them the opportunity to do so through his management of the game. There is nothing more frustrating than to referee a match in which the players continuously fail to make the best of their chances: it is only human nature to feel that you as the referee have also failed in some way. But good referees know that they will not always be able to improve the standard of a game. As long as they have made every effort to create and sustain the right conditions, there is nothing more that can be asked of them.

The referee is therefore a manager. He knows the theory and purpose of the Laws, and on the pitch it is his duty to apply and interpret those Laws for the proper management of the game. He is also a facilitator. At the most basic level, his presence allows the two teams to play, but there is much more to it than that. By applying his skill, knowledge and experience, the referee gives the players an opportunity to perform to the best of their abilities - whether they do or not is none of his concern, but he must create the platform for all 30 players to do the best they can. A referee who does not apply the Law of Advantage properly is failing in his duty as a facilitator, for example, as is one who misses encroachments beyond the offside line or boring in the front row. The good referee facilitates the game by spotting and penalising destructive tactics and encouraging and rewarding constructive play.

A useful checklist of management skills is as follows.

- Demonstration of an empathy for the game by letting it develop in accordance with the temper of the match.
- Management of verbal interactions with players so that it is evident that the referee is clear and confident.
- Identification and management of flash-points (e.g. bodies on the ground, problems at set-pieces, persistent offences).
- Avoidance of foul play originating from a lack of management in critical phases of play.
- Management of foul play and persistent infringement with appropriate action as required.
- Management of situations without resorting to penalties, except in situations where players do not respond.
- Demonstration of an intent to provide solutions to problems so that the same offences are not penalised throughout the game.
- Maintenance of concentration throughout the game.
- Confident decision making which is unaffected by the pace of the game, crowd or player pressure (especially when making difficult decisions which could have a major bearing on the outcome of the game).

When a game is managed well, the referee clearly establishes credible relationships with the two teams. He sets clear priorities and is consistent in his application of the Laws. In keeping with his mandate, the good referee will always try to resolve problems early so that the game is not spoilt through persistent infringements which could have been obviated. An important point to note is that the referee only really gets one chance to impose his authority: how he behaves in the first ten minutes will determine the subsequent temper and nature of the game, so it's critical that the referee is consistent, firm and fair from the kick-off. Players want to know where they stand immediately, and it's the referee's duty to set those standards from the start.

(2) The basic principles

As an overriding priority, the referee has to abide by three fundamental principles: **safety, equity, and Laws.**

(2.1) Safety

Rugby is a physically demanding sport. Quite apart from the obvious contact elements, there is now a much greater demand on fitness levels as the Laws have evolved to increase the speed and openness of the game. This combination may lead to situations where the referee will have to intervene to ensure the safety of the players involved.

It is therefore the referee's primary responsibility to ensure the safety of all players at all times. The players' safety takes precedence over everything else: **if it looks dangerous, stop it**. The good referee never compromises safety, and will be constantly alert to potential dangers - body positions in the tackle, scrummage, line-out, ruck and maul - and use the whistle to prevent injury. A referee can always justify a decision to stop the progress of a game on the grounds of safety.

It cannot be stressed too often that the primary role of the referee is to protect the players. You cannot always protect them from themselves, if they are determined to place themselves in danger, but you must be there to make sure that they are protected from the consequences of their actions, however injudicious they may have been. Foul and dangerous play have no place in the game and, as the RFU says, the Laws provide all the necessary sanctions - as well as preventive measures - to allow a fair physical contest.

To attain this level of protection, the referee has numerous additional duties. The referee is not a policeman, nor is he the Lawmaker. The referee is described in the Laws as the sole judge of fact and of Law; in other words, his decisions are final (with the proviso that he can change his decision based on information given to him by his touch judges). But referees do not want to be seen solely as judges, nor do the players wish to treat them as such. Referring back to that earlier statement of the referee's objective, he is there to manage an environment in which both sides can play and enjoy the game within the Laws.

(2.2) Equity

Players rightly assume that referees appointed to their games will be impartial, consistent and fair. This is the basic principle of equity. To apply this principle, referees need to demonstrate that they understand the game and have an empathy with the players and what they are trying to achieve. Applying the principle involves the following key elements of referee behaviour.

- He will be consistent, even-handed and fair.
- He will be firm, yet friendly and approachable.
- He will be positive and take control.
- He will set standards early and vigilantly maintain them.
- He will treat players sympathetically.
- He will play advantage to the full (other than for reasons of safety).
- He will take up positions which give him the best all-round view of the game.

This list seems daunting, especially when you consider some of the research on referees. On average, it has been estimated that a referee will make over 1,000 decisions during a game - a number that includes all those decisions not to blow the whistle. The referee will cover over four miles during a game, and 13% of that distance will be with backwards movement. Even during set pieces, referees are rarely still. As they are engaged in all this activity, they have to be thinking about the application of the Laws and the safety of the players. They also have to bear in mind that they must treat all 30 players exactly the same, and that the players will have seen how the referee interprets their actions and what response he gives. Once a precedent is set, it must be followed, because that is what the players on both sides want and expect.

(2.3) Laws

Naturally, the referee must know and understand the Laws. The Law book is a start, but it is by no means the end. If you simply learn the Laws without ever bothering to understand the motives behind them, you will always have a problem managing your games.

Many referees like to study a different Law every week; they will take each part of it and visualise situations in which its application will or might be relevant. The skill of visualisation is something that will only come after a little experience with the whistle, but it is a skill that is well worth developing. It is vital that referees are able to translate the intentions of the Lawmakers into practical decision making. Good interpretation of the Laws is something that only comes with practice, and the good referee never stops learning.

(3) Communication

However good you may be as a referee, your qualities count for nothing if you cannot communicate. You must let the players know what you expect, and explain your decisions clearly and suc-cinctly. Remember that the players are under your management on the pitch, and they need you to tell them how to behave.

Each referee develops his own style of communication, and it must be natural. You're there to let the players enjoy the game, and they want you to be decisive, firm yet approachable. The referee has to have a rapport with the players so that they trust him and will accept his decisions without dissent. There are as many different ways of achieving this as there are referees, and you must be com-fortable with your own. Listen to what other referees say, and watch how they communicate; study videos of the top games, and go and watch your local side and see how the referee behaves. You will only know what's best for you once you're on the field, but you can learn some valuable lessons from others. Do not try and copy others, but adapt their better habits to suit yourself.

A cautionary note on communication: do not, under any circum-stances, swear or use foul language. This immediately demon-strates to the players that you have lost control, and you will find it much more difficult to retain their respect for you. You earn that respect by staying calm; losing your temper, however trying the situation, is the quickest way of causing irreparable harm to the management of the game.

Communicating with the players comes in three ways: **voice, whistle and body.**

(3.1) The voice

The best referees talk to players all the time, preventing infringements and advising players on the correct course of action. But players will always make mistakes, and some will try to overstep the boundaries in the hope that the referee doesn't spot them. This is the area where discretion plays such a vital role in the referee's skill set: spotting an infringement doesn't necessarily mandate whistling for it, especially if the non-infringing team gains an advantage. 'I saw what you did, Red 8, and don't do it again', is a very effective method of communicating without breaking up the flow of the game and denying advantage to the opposition.

Using clear oral communication is therefore vital to let players know what is and is not allowed in Law: 'Penalty kick to Red. Blue 2, you joined the maul in front of the hindmost player. You're offside.' One of the better acronyms to bear in mind is **ATP** - Advise, Tell, Penalise. Infringing players who are not interfering with play can be advised of what they're doing wrong, told once more if they repeat the offence, then penalised if they still haven't got the message. Obviously this doesn't apply to every situation, especially when foul play is involved, but it gets the message across without blowing for every infringement. Nobody wants to participate in a game where the referee blows for every incident, regardless of its bearing on the result.

The voice can and should be used to prevent offences occurring, for example: 'Stay onside, 6. Release the ball. Roll away.' Players respond well to a referee who talks to them. The players don't want to have to guess what the referee is looking for, and what is or is not acceptable. If they have those parameters established for them, through clear and consistent instructions from the referee, they can concentrate on playing the game. In many games you'll find that the referee is almost constantly talking during the first 15 to 20 minutes, setting out his requirements straight away and managing the players so that they don't consistently infringe. But consistent chattering does not help the players if there is no purpose to it. Verbal communications must have a clear objective behind them: to prevent or to explain an infringement.

The tone of voice used should be firm and positive, indicating that the referee is in control and will not accept any nonsense. The referee doesn't want to sound officious and out of touch, but needs to convey confidence and a sympathy with his players. Talk is always the preferred first option; the whistle should only be used when players choose not to listen.

(3.2) The whistle

You might think that the whistle is a somewhat crude and inflexible instrument, but it is actually remarkably versatile. Referee advisers will say that, when they are watching a good referee, they can stand with their backs to play and still know what the referee has blown for, so distinct are the different signals. A very loud and long blast will signify foul play; a loud blast for a penalty or a try; medium for the award of a scrummage; and light for ball in touch or a conversion. The old adage of refereeing is: 'Think quick, blow slow.' The whistle should never be held in the mouth, but should be securely wrapped around the hand with a bootlace or with elastic.

(3.3) The body

What about the body? The right body language is critical to the success of a referee. It includes how the referee is turned out: are the boots and kit clean, the hair neat, all the accoutrements (pencil, whistle, score-card, yellow/red cards, handkerchief) in good working order? Does he look fit to referee? It even extends beyond the pitch to the clubhouse: how does the referee look before and after the game? Does he arrive looking smart? Is he confident when he walks in before the match, and how does he look when he goes for a drink with the players after the game? We'll cover these aspects in more detail later in this chapter, but the referee needs to create the right aura from the minute he arrives.

On the pitch, of course, the body plays a major part. The correct signals (*see* pp.105-15) need to be given clearly and crisply, so that all the players and spectators can see what is going on. Even if a referee is making all the right decisions, it is very frustrating if some of the players - or spectators - are unable to understand those decisions. Hand signals give the first indication of what the infringement was and against whom the decision is made. There is no room for customisation or flamboyance; as long as the signals are properly made, and visible to all interested parties, there should be nothing to complain about. Bear in mind that the size of a referee is important here: a tall referee has an advantage, and shorter ones need to ensure that their signals can be clearly seen, especially when they are surrounded by giant locks and flankers!

The general rule is that the visual signal will be the first indication by the referee of what has happened and what is going to happen: whistle; signal; explain. When there is a breakdown in open play, there may only be four or five players in earshot of the referee, so he needs to signal the reason for the stoppage before other players have arrived. Then he can say, for example: 'Knock on by Red 6. Scrum here. Blue ball.'

Time is at a premium, and yet the best referees seem to have a lot of it. They read the game so that they're always in the right position; they are never hurried, and always have the time to look around so that they are not solely concentrating on where the ball is. Whilst much of this comes from experience and fitness, and new referees cannot expect to do this from the start, players react positively to those referees who give the appearance of complete control. By being in the right place, and using a quick movement of the head to look back and see what's happening behind you, you win the players' respect. The backs don't know for sure if you've seen them creeping offside at a ruck, but an arm outstretched after one of these rapid glances can often achieve the desired effect, and they may not be tempted to try and gain an unfair advantage.

(4) The team of three

Unfortunately, the role of the touch judge is much maligned and misunderstood. Far from being someone who is pulled from the bar to wave a grubby handkerchief from time to time, the touch judge is a vital assistant to the referee and can have a major influence on the game.

Law 6 states that: *There shall be two touch judges for every match. Unless touch judges have been appointed by or under the authority of the Union, it shall be the responsibility of each team to provide a touch judge.* This is a part of the Laws which is rarely applied at the lower levels of the game, and junior referees tend to regard touch judges as something of a luxury. However, it is useful to learn about the management of touch judges and the way in which the team of three can work together to create a better game.

For the concept to work well, the referee has to brief the touch judges fully on what he wants and expects from them. Apart from the obvious priorities of marking touch and judging kicks at goal, tough judges appointed by a Society or the RFU can also help the referee to spot infringements in all the critical phases of play, and can mark out onside/offside lines for the players. There are recommended hand signals for foul play, offside, front row scrummage offences and knock-ons, and the referee should know these signals.

15

He can instruct the touch judges to perform a variety of duties, including keeping the score and the time and monitoring play in-goal, but he must not assume that his touch judges will know what he wants them to do. The pre-match briefing is therefore an important part of the referee's preparation.

Management of the team of three is in the hands of the referee, and his success is judged on the following criteria.

- Evidence of thorough briefing of touch judges.
- Foul play situations managed jointly.
- Evidence of communication and teamwork between the referee and touch judges.
- Referee supportive of touch judges.
- Demonstration of an ability to react to touch judge advisory signals.

Used effectively, touch judges add two pairs of eyes and ears to the management of the game and can draw the referee's attention to situations that might otherwise not be noticed and addressed. The referee remains the sole judge of fact and Law, but he can and should involve his touch judges to give him additional vision and coverage.

(5) Preparation

For any activity to be a success, it requires good preparation. Contrary to how it may look, the referee's job extends way beyond the 80 minutes he spends on the pitch every Saturday. Referees invest a significant part of their time in other activities separate from, but related to, the actual game. They train; they study; they teach others; they act as ambassadors; and they prepare themselves for each appointment.

(5.1) Advance planning

The referee who belongs to a Society will normally receive a monthly list of appointments, detailing the home side, the opposition, the time and the venue. This is when the referee starts his preparation: he needs to organise his transport, for instance, as well as thinking about the nature of each fixture. Is it a cup game, a friendly, a league match, an under-19 game? In the week before the fixture he will be contacted by the home club's fixtures secretary to confirm the details. This is the first opportunity the referee has to set his standards; in effect, the fixture starts with this call. The referee can and should ask about first aid facilities, touch judges (if none are appointed), the name of the captain, the precise location and phone number of the clubhouse, and the colours of both sides. If he needs to be picked up from the station, he should arrange it there and then. In this conversation he can convey his authority and his competence before he's even stepped on the pitch.

Once he has this information, the referee can start to plan. This will begin with his kit. All the kit needs to be clean and in good condition. The boots and their laces should be spotless. He will need three shirts - of completely different plain colours - and three pairs of shorts (white, black and navy blue) and socks. If he plans to warm up outside, he should have a track suit and trainers. It's easy to forget to pack a towel and toiletries; these are important because he needs to look as smart in the bar afterwards as he did when he arrived.

The referee carries an increasingly large number of accoutrements. Many referees have a special box in which they store it all.

- Two whistles (Acme Thunderers are recommended).
- Two sharpened, short pencils.
- Score-cards (with a waterproof holder so that they don't get sodden in the rain).
- Yellow and red cards.
- Stud measure, spare studs, and stud key.
- Clean handkerchief (useful for removing mud and dirt from players' eyes).
- Coin for the toss.
- Sock garters.
- Spare laces.
- Two watches (preferably with stop-watch and/or count-down facility).
- The Law book.

Do not rely upon anyone else to put your kit together, and keep on checking that you've got everything so that you're not faced with a last minute panic when you can't find a clean pair of socks. If you belong to a Referee Society which uses grading cards for feedback from the clubs on referee performance, these should be filled out as much as possible before you leave home (and put a stamp on them), but bear in mind that, in more junior games, the opposition some-times turns out to be different to that expected, or you may be asked to cover a different fixture at the last minute.

(5.2) The right diet

Referees have lots of problems with their eating schedule before a game. When you run on the field, if your glycogen levels are low your capacity to maintain the necessary work rate for 80 minutes will be impaired, so how you have eaten during the days prior to the game will have an influence.

It's therefore desirable to have an adequate intake of carbohydrate in preparation for a match. In the week leading up to a game, and especially the last couple of days, there should be an increased carbohydrate intake. But this does not mean that you should stuff yourself! There should be a gradual increase in carbohydrate and fluid throughout the week. Take smaller, more frequent high carbohydrate meals which are easier on the stomach. Last minute stockpiling is harmful rather than helpful, so the meal on Friday evening should be relatively light.

Any meal on match day should ideally be taken a good 3 to 4 hours before kick-off to allow plenty of time for digestion. One important reason for this is that anxiety tends to slow down the rate at which food moves through the system. The meal should be light, easily digestible and consist mainly of carbohydrates. Fluid intake is obviously very important and must be maintained.

(5.3) Match day procedure

As a general rule, the more senior the game, the earlier you should arrive at the ground. In any event, you need to plan an early arrival to give yourself plenty of time to get in the right physical and mental state, and to attend to some important pre-match issues. Look the part - a referee who arrives wearing a blazer, Society tie and smart trousers and shoes will immediately create a more favourable impression than one who turns up looking dishevelled and disorganised. Additionally, you'll be instantly recognisable as the referee if you're smartly dressed.

If an adviser has been assigned to your game he will introduce himself to you as early as possible and will then leave you be. He understands that this pre-match period is stressful and that you have other concerns; remember that he's been through it himself. Do not worry about the presence of an adviser; as his title suggests, he's there to help you improve your game, not hurl criticism at you. If you have been given qualified touch judges, you must make contact with them early and give them clear instructions as to what you require from them.

At the lower levels both team captains may be struggling to find 15 players, and they will appreciate knowing that they have one less thing to worry about if they have a referee. Introduce yourself to the home captain; ask to see the first aid box and stretcher, and find out if there is a qualified medical representative on site. You should also arrange a time to do the stud and dress check. Some teams like to go out and warm up before returning to the changing room for a final briefing, whilst others do not come back. Ask both skippers what their routine is, and tell them exactly when you want to do the check - in the changing room is preferable to out on the field. You should also try to arrange the toss before they go out.

At this stage you can also request touch judges but, especially with junior sides, be prepared that you will not have any. If that is the case, tell both captains that you are there to referee, not run touch, so that they understand your role and expectations. You should also confirm the kick-off time to avoid any misunderstanding. Be friendly but keep your discussion with the captains to the point; they don't want to be bothered with you any more than is necessary.

If, as is often the case, there is no separate changing room for officials and you are asked to share with the home team, make sure you leave enough time to change before the team comes in. They need their privacy and they won't want you encroaching on it. If necessary, change immediately and go out; the players will appreciate your sensitivity.

Your first task outside is to inspect the pitch. Is it properly marked out? Are there overhanging trees or other obstructions? If there is more than one pitch, do the lines run parallel to each other or are there overlaps? How deep are the in-goal areas? Are they the same at both ends? Are all the required flags in place? Are there post protectors, and are the posts themselves secure? Where is the sun, and will it get in your eyes and affect your vision? As you inspect the pitch you should be walking off the journey and getting yourself attuned to the task ahead. This is often the time when referees feel most stress, and many like to have a set routine which deals with it. Develop your own schedule, but don't make it so hard and fast that, if anything changes, your confidence will be adversely affected.

(5.4) Dealing with stress

Everyone copes with stress in a different way. As you become more experienced you will learn how to live with it more effectively, but it is perfectly healthy and normal to have some level of stress. It helps to think about what you are trying to achieve, and what your priorities should be. Some referees can visualise situations that may occur during the game and how they will handle them. The major priorities will always run along similar lines.

- **General** - to prevent flash-points in which players become involved in foul play.
- **Open play** - to keep players on their feet and onside.
- **Scrummage** - to keep the scrummage up, both for safety reasons and to get the ball back into play as quickly and cleanly as possible.
- **Line-out** - to concentrate on offences across the line-out, because they tend to be destructive.
- **Rucks and mauls** - to keep players on their feet and to restrict infringements, i.e. straying offside.

Concentrating on these basic priorities will help you to prepare psychologically. There are also useful relaxation techniques to assist in dealing with anxiety. When nervous or apprehensive, there is a tendency to breathe quickly and not deeply enough. The part of the breathing process that is frequently performed incorrectly is exhaling. In order to acquire the optimum amount of oxygen for the system to stimulate awareness and brain functions, the following exercises are recommended.

(1) **This exercise can be used at any time prior to kick-off to ensure that the anxiety level is at the optimal level.**
- Breathe out quite strongly to exhale all the stale air from the lungs.
- Breathe in and hold the breath for a count of eight.
- Let the air exhale gently.
- Wait for a count of five and see if your finger-tips tingle slightly, which indicates that oxygen is circulating well in the blood stream. At this point you should begin to feel relaxed yet alert.

(2) **This exercise is longer term and will generate deep relaxation, so it is not useful immediately before a game but very good in the days preceding a game or on the morning of the game.**
- Close your eyes and focus the mind on your toes and be aware of how they feel. Tense the feet slightly and then release the tension.
- Carry out the same procedure with calves, thighs and stomach, working up through the body to include the face and scalp.
- Finish by focussing on your breathing and noticing that it is slow and even. When you are ready, open your eyes and experience the feeling of calm and well-being which results from this exercise.

(5.5) Final preparation

When you are back in the changing room, check your kit again and lay out everything you will need to take with you. If you know that you will have to travel some distance to the pitch, be sure to pack your spares to take with you - no-one wants the game held up while you race back to the changing room for a new pencil.

Once you are changed, check again on the two teams to see if they are going to have full sides; you should be especially concerned about the front rows, as you will need to play uncontested scrummages if either side cannot raise a qualified front row.

At this stage you should go through your own physical routine, stretching and exercising to get the muscles warm and ready for action. Your warm-up needs to be fairly close to kick-off time so that you don't lose the benefits.

An effective warm-up.
(1) Gentle jog for 3-5 minutes (including jogging backwards and sideways).
(2) High knee raises for 15-20 metres, walk back and repeat four times. Bring the knees up higher than parallel to the ground; pick up speed of movement; try to maintain the knee lift; don't tense up; stay relaxed.
(3) Flicks for 15-20 metres, walk back and repeat four times. Flick heels up quickly to seat; leave your hands by your side and allow feet to tap hands each time; keep body upright.
(4) Sprint for 20 metres, walk back and repeat five times. Start by striding out at approximately three-quarters pace and progressively increase pace with each sprint

The warm-up should also include some stretching, either after or in between the suggested activities. It is equally advisable to warm down after a training session or game to help the adaptations which the body has to bring about in the recovery phase. This can be done with mild, rhythmic muscular activity, such as jogging or skipping, which gradually decreases in intensity. Stretching is also recommended.

Your final action before going out to the pitch should be the stud and dress check. The Laws are very precise about what is, and what is not, allowed, and you must adhere to these strictures for the players' safety. Some referees do a roaring trade in selling legal studs to players before the game! If you have the resources, carry spare studs with you so that you can help the players.

With regard to dress, there is a fine line to be drawn. Referees are not expected to frisk every player and check their hands for rings, and you must put the onus on the players to show you if they think they're wearing something that might be illegal. Warn them of the consequences if they do not do this; Law 4 (Players' Dress) authorises the referee to send off a player who is wearing an illegal item. Law 6 (Referee and Touch Judges) forbids the referee from giving *any instruction or advice to either team prior to the match.* However, you must exercise a degree of discretion about this. Whilst you have all the players together in the changing room you have your first opportunity to tell them of your expectations. By reminding them to stay on their feet, and onside, you are taking preventive measures - if they don't comply during the game, they have only themselves to blame. Additionally, telling the front rows how you will set the scrummage could avoid problems later on. Be aware that many players have never seen a Law book, so if they ask questions, especially at the beginning of the season when there may be new Law changes, try to be helpful without compromising yourself. There's another good reason for talking to the players before the game: it gets them used to your voice, which they'll be hearing a lot on the pitch. If you have touch judges, make sure they talk to the players as well - they, too, will be communicating during the game and the players need to know how they sound. Finally, whatever you have said, remember to wish them good luck and a good game.

Expect the sides to be out on time and ready for the kick-off as scheduled, but exercise a degree of tolerance in junior matches where the sides may be still be struggling to raise a full 15. It's much better to wait five minutes for a prop to arrive than to kick off without him.

(6) After the game

You will experience the full gamut of emotions after a game. When you have finished your first one, the major feeling will be one of enormous relief that it's all over. As you get more experience you become more critical, and you tend to focus on the things that did not go as well as you'd hoped. There may have been particular incidents which unsettled you - a sending off, a disallowed try, a collapsed scrum, a bad injury - or an area of the Laws which you didn't manage very effectively. As you warm down, or pull off your boots, thoughts of these will undoubtedly dominate. Very few referees come back to the changing room with the feeling that they have achieved everything they'd planned. That's human nature, and it's hard to fight against it. After all, you will only improve your skills if you are constructively critical of your own performance.

You may have little time for quiet reflection, especially if you're sharing a changing room with one of the teams. The players will be talking about the game, and some of their remarks may be designed to wind you up. Keep your counsel: an unguarded response to some criticism from a player may be very damaging, not just for you but for every referee who subsequently comes to the club. Don't loiter in the changing room; take your shower early and let the players relax and unwind without you inhibiting their discussion. It is, however, very important that you make yourself available to all the players after the game. There are two main reasons for this.

Firstly, you can help the players by discussing their concerns and improving their understanding of the Laws. Very often they will want clarification of a point of Law - when does a line-out end, for example? - and you should discuss this with them without getting into the details of every decision you made. You will also learn much from this discussion: you'll find out how they interpret the Laws, and possibly how other referees have approached similar issues (although you must never comment on another referee's performance). One other word of warning: never produce a Law book in the bar. The decisions you make on the pitch are final, and that's that; don't let yourself get compromised by too much debate on specific issues related to the game. Don't be afraid to admit to mistakes: the players know you're only human, and you'll be much better regarded if you demonstrate this! Secondly, remember that rugby is still predominantly a social sport, played for pleasure rather than gain. The after-match drinks in the bar are usually friendly and fun, and the referee, as part of the game, should participate - even if he only drinks orange juice and lemonade! You do not want the players to think that you're unapproachable and superior - either on or off the pitch.

If you have been watched by an adviser, he will be waiting for you in the club bar. He'll be sympathetic about you needing to mix with the players, and he'll try and fit in his session with you around that. He'll find a quiet corner for you both to go through his assessment of your performance, and to discuss any problems or questions you may have. Don't waste the opportunity to talk with an adviser - he's seen it all and can offer an enormous amount of practical advice.

You must make sure that you thank both captains for the game and, where appropriate, anyone from the club who ran the line or helped you in other ways. If the game was a competitive fixture you will probably be asked to sign team sheets and confirm the score. Once you've done all this, you're free to go home.

(7) Fit to referee

Fitness is not an absolute state. It is relative, and comes in many different forms. The rugby player requires different fitness attributes to, say, a squash player or a boxer. The pace of rugby union has changed so dramatically over the last decade that there are no longer any hiding places for the unfit; the game has developed to such an extent that today's top forwards are almost as quick and mobile as backs were ten years ago. Progressive Law changes have succeeded in making a faster game with rapid recycling of the ball and fewer stoppages. The demands of competitive, open rugby - in league and international fixtures - have highlighted the need for much higher levels of fitness.

As the 31st player on the pitch, the referee's fitness has also assumed much more importance. With so much at stake in competitive matches, the responsibility of the referee to keep up with play has greatly increased. It is no longer acceptable to make judgements some 15 or 20 metres from the ball. Whilst fitness alone cannot guarantee a better standard of refereeing, it certainly allows the referee a better opportunity of being in the best position to make correct decisions. Those who have come to refereeing because they could no longer maintain their fitness level for playing are in for a rude shock! (There is more information on the whole subject of fitness and diet in the RFU's booklet, 'Fit to Referee and Touch Judge'.)

(7.1) The basics of fitness

For the purposes of the rugby referee, fitness can be broken down into six different elements.

- **Aerobic endurance** is the capacity of a referee to maintain continuous activity over a long period of time.
- **Muscular endurance** represents the capacity for continuous performance of relatively localised muscular activity.
- **Strength** is the capacity to exert a force against a resistance, ranging from explosive, powerful movements to more statically applied strength.
- **Speed** is the ability to run fast, to accelerate, to change direction and react quickly.

- **Flexibility** is the freedom to move the body through a wide range of motions and positions.
- **Agility** involves speed of movement, and a change of direction, in a controlled, balanced way.

Before getting into the detail of how to achieve and maintain these components, we should consider the basics of fitness. One important principle of physiological fitness is that the major body systems - in particular the heart, lungs and circulation (known as the cardio-vascular system) - benefit from being challenged. This system is very trainable and it thrives from operating at higher levels. This is what separates humans from machines: the body can adapt and improve its efficiency as a result of work.

The basis to fitness training is endurance, which ensures that the muscles can call on enough energy to enable them to keep working and delay the onset of fatigue. The two vital factors in the provision of energy are **oxygen supply** and **nutrition.**

Oxygen is brought into the body by the lungs, and transported in the blood, which is pumped round the body by the heart. Energy is supplied in the body by several systems. One of these is the aerobic system, in which energy is produced in the presence of oxygen (aerobic means with oxygen). This energy system is important for continuous work, for keeping going for 80 minutes. It is a long term energy supply. But the aerobic system often fails to meet the needs of referees during the game, especially when they have to perform several hard sprints with only brief periods of rest. Although the aerobic system is a vital and efficient energy system, it is often unable to supply energy at a sufficiently high rate, such as in a sprint, so additional energy is supplied by the anaerobic systems.

One of these anaerobic systems, glycolysis, uses glycogen stored in the muscle to deliver rapid energy and, over a short period of time, this system can supply enough energy to cope with very intensive work. The problem is that lactic acid is also released which is a cause of fatigue in the body, and eventually the need to slow down or stop becomes apparent. With the right kind of training - e.g. shuttle running - the body's tolerance to lactic acid can be raised.

Referees can also improve their fitness through strength work. Although referees do not need the same high levels of strength and power as players, they should work on appropriate strength training programmes to develop qualities such as muscular endurance and acceleration.

There is another aspect to physical fitness: *Mens sana in corpore sano* (A healthy mind in a healthy body). If you are physically fit, your mental faculties are much sharper. When you arrive at a break-down in open play, and a ruck or maul develops, you need to be alert to all the potential infringements. If you're unfit, you'll find yourself struggling to make those decisions: you'll be too tired, and too concerned with your own recovery, to give your full attention to the game. But if you're in good physical condition, you'll have one less thing to worry about.

(7.2) Principles of training

You cannot hope to get and stay fit simply by refereeing on a Saturday afternoon; you can, however, train the body and energy systems in advance so that the 80 minutes you spend on the pitch are not too unpleasant and painful. To achieve any increase in fitness, the referee has to train a little harder - the principle of overload. For training to have any impact, it must overload the system sensibly. When that happens, the body adapts to the load, so that what was once exceptional becomes standard. Subtle changes in the body take place as it adapts to the added demands imposed on it; but the body adapts slowly and any attempt to rush the process may well result in injury, illness or both.

The principle of adaptation works by making demands where intensity and duration force the body to adjust its performance upwards. This increases the body's tolerance for more activity of even greater intensity. The improvement is not a straight line on a graph: individuals have different tolerances, and the degree of intensity or severity of the exercise must be varied accordingly as the training progresses.

This progression needs a careful and sensible build-up of training over weeks and months, stage by stage. If the training loads are increased too quickly the body will not be able to adapt. On the other side of the coin, there is the problem of reversibility. Any improvement in fitness is purely temporary. Fitness is hard to gain and easy to lose, so it's important to maintain fitness work on a regular basis.

Finally, the fitness regime needs to be varied. If the same exercises are carried out day after day then boredom and staleness will soon set in. Variation of exercise and training regimes will maintain motivation and interest. It also helps to train with someone else - many referees work with their local rugby club.

(7.3) Fitness programmes

As we've already noted, fitness is subjective and has to be built around the demands and needs of the individual, so it is inappropriate to set out lists of training schedules. There are, however, some basic principles that apply to all referees.

- Start your endurance training during the summer, aiming for four sessions a week - you must be fit when the season starts or you'll never catch up.
- Develop a programme that is appropriate - take advice from professionals.
- By the start of the season you should be doing two endurance sessions and one speed session in addition to your matches.
- Remember that speed is just as vital as stamina - you must work on your sprinting.
- Swimming, squash, tennis, etc. are all good forms of exercise which are also enjoyable - use them as part of your programme.
- Don't overdo it at first - build up sensibly. As we get older the body takes more time to adapt, and more time to recover.
- Vary the weekly routine to maintain your interest and to develop different fitness attributes.
- Don't forget warm-up/warm-down sessions - many injuries occur because these are not properly carried out.

(7.4) Nutrition and diet

We have probably all heard of the business acronym GIGO - 'Garbage In, Garbage Out'. This can equally apply to diet: if you eat badly then your body will respond accordingly. Whilst no-one wishes to be a slave to refereeing, there are some sensible guidelines for eating that will enhance performance and help your body to recover between exercise sessions.

We know that improvements in fitness are the result of the body adapting to the stresses of training. This adaptation requires that the body takes in all the necessary nutrients, so you must pay attention to your eating habits 365 days of the year - not just on those few days prior to games. To ensure that your diet meets the demands placed on your body, you should consume sufficient energy in the form of **carbohydrates** so that you can maintain the stores of energy within the muscles.

Carbohydrates are stored within the muscle in the form of glycogen. As mentioned earlier, glycogen is released by the muscles to deliver rapid energy when there is an oxygen deficit. You can only replace it by eating or drinking substances that contain carbohydrates. The emphasis should be on complex carbohydrates: bread, potatoes, rice, pasta, pulses, cereals, vegetables (especially root vegetables and green leafy vegetables), fresh fruit (apples, bananas, oranges) and dried fruit (apricots, prunes).

Try to reduce the overall amount of fat in your diet. Start off by decreasing consumption of all visible fat (butter, lard, oils, meat fat) and non-visible fat (milk, dairy produce, eggs, mayonnaise, sausages, pâté, pies and pastry). In contrast to carbohydrates, fat cannot be used as an immediate energy supply.

Finally, ensure that you maintain a high fluid intake by drinking plenty of water and fresh fruit juice as part of your normal diet.

(8) Foul play

We now come to the most difficult part of game management - Law 26. Foul play is, happily, a rare occurrence in the game of rugby union, largely because coaches and referees have worked very hard to convince players that it is unacceptable; additionally, the disciplinary committees have wide discretion to impose hefty suspensions on players who are found guilty of foul play.

However, this is not an area for complacency: eventually, every referee has to deal with a foul play situation and it needs to be handled with equal measures of firmness, diplomacy and pragmatism. You should always bear in mind, with this Law as with all others, that the onus on compliance lies with the players - especially the captains - and the coaches. The Laws clearly set out the parameters, and you are there to see that the game is conducted within those parameters, but you must not take sole responsibility for ensuring that the game is played in a sporting spirit. Captains also carry a heavy responsibility for the discipline of their sides, as do the coaches, and you will occasionally need to remind them of that.

(8.1) The authority of the referee

Before getting into the details of foul play and how to handle it, there is one other Law which is particularly relevant: Law 6, Referee and Touch Judges. Law 6 is important because it lays down some unequivocal statements about the referee's authority. For example: *During a match the referee is the sole judge of fact and of Law. All his decisions are binding on the players ... All players must respect the authority of the referee and they must not dispute his decisions. They must (except in the case of a kick-off) stop playing at once when the referee has blown his whistle.* Offences by players under Law 6 are to be treated as misconduct, and dealt with under the provisions of Law 26. This means that dissent is normally penalised with a penalty kick; however, if the dissent follows the award of a penalty kick, the referee has the power to advance the mark of the kick a further 10 metres. If the original penalty was a free kick, the referee can change this to a penalty kick as a result of dissent from the offending team. He can also reverse a decision if there is dissent. Law 6 therefore establishes the authority of the referee, but do not confuse this with respect: that has to earnt from the players.

(8.2) Foul play infringements

Basically, actions of foul play can be divided into two categories - those that endanger the safety of other players, and those that are contrary to the Laws and spirit of the game.

(8.2.1) Dangerous play

Remembering the referee's primary duty to ensure the safety of all the players, dangerous play must be severely penalised. Dangerous play includes the following.

- Early and late tackles.
- Striking, hacking, kicking, tripping or trampling on an opponent.
- Charging or obstructing an opponent who has just kicked the ball.
- Holding, pushing, charging, obstructing or grasping an opponent not holding the ball (except in a scrummage, ruck or maul).
- Forming the scrummage some distance from the opponents and rushing against them on engagement.
- Lifting opponents in the front row of a scrummage.
- Collapsing a scrummage, ruck or maul.

Guidance to referees is unequivocal: *A player guilty of dangerous play shall either be ordered off or else cautioned that he will be ordered off if he repeats the offence.* There certainly appears to be no room for doubt here, and yet the referee has to make critical decisions - with help from his touch judges, if present - on what constitutes dangerous play and what is merely accidental or clumsy. Some of the Law's definitions of dangerous play include the word 'wilfully': this suggests that the referee needs to interpret the intention of the player when deciding on the nature of the infringement. For instance, a ruck forms in which there are bodies on the ground, and a player joins the ruck and, in attempting to get his boot on the ball, rakes a grounded player with his studs. Is it intentional or accidental? Only the referee can decide and, in reaching that decision, much weight must be given to the temper of the game.

There should, however, be no differentiation between wilful and reckless behaviour. If a player acts in a reckless way, so that his action is likely to endanger others, he should be punished without regard for intent. Dangerous play, however initiated and for whatever reason, must be dealt with strictly.

The best advice is obviously to prevent potential flash-points. Experienced referees exercise their judgement on the temper of the game and manage it accordingly. If, for example, the game clearly has the potential for violence - a local derby, a critical cup battle or a vital league match - the referee is likely to be particularly firm so that the players understand that dangerous play will not be tolerated. Cautions are one method of controlling the behaviour of players, as they send a message to all the players that the referee is in charge and will not allow dangerous play to go unpunished. Referees who do not adhere to this policy are doing a disservice to all the players, coaches, spectators and other referees. It is recommended that all referees study the RFU booklet on Law 26, which includes a number of case studies and guidance on how to manage foul play.

(8.2.2) Other foul play

There are four other actions which constitute foul play: obstruction, unfair play, misconduct and repeated infringements.

Obstruction basically occurs when one player, who is not carrying the ball, interferes with another illegally.

This includes:
- charging or pushing an opponent running for the ball (except shoulder to shoulder)
- being in an offside position (i.e. in front of the ball) and running or standing in front of a team-mate carrying the ball, thus shielding him from opponents
- taking the ball from a scrummage, ruck, maul or line-out and running back into his own players
- as a back-row player, changing body position at a scrummage to prevent an opponent moving round the scrummage.

All these infringements result in a penalty kick (or a penalty try).

Unfair play is unsportsmanlike conduct, and includes the following.

- Deliberately playing unfairly, or wilfully infringing any Law of the game (penalty kick).
- Wilfully wasting time (free kick).
- Wilfully knocking or throwing the ball from the playing area into touch, touch-in-goal or over the dead-ball line (free kick).

Misconduct is a catch-all infringement, and is probably the most common reason for cautions and dismissals. Law 26 is deliberately broad in its definition of misconduct, stating it is illegal for any player to do the following.

- While the ball is out of play to molest, obstruct, or in any way interfere with an opponent or be guilty of any form of misconduct.
- To commit any misconduct on the playing area which is prejudicial to the spirit of good sportsmanship.

In addition to a penalty kick or penalty try, infringements of misconduct must result in a caution or dismissal.

Repeated infringement is self-explanatory, and results in a penalty kick and, if necessary, a caution and subsequent dismissal.

(8.3) Dealing with foul play

Law 26 gives a very broad definition: *Foul Play is any action by a player which is contrary to the letter and spirit of the Game and includes obstruction, unfair play, misconduct, dangerous play, unsporting behaviour, retaliation and repeated infringements.* These actions nearly always result in a penalty kick, or penalty try, in favour of the non-infringing team. However, Law 26 also gives the referee the power to caution players for offences committed under this Law, and to order them off.

Some people say that the referee has somehow failed in his duty if he needs to resort to cautions and dismissals. This is completely wrong: it is one of the referee's primary duties to ensure that players guilty of foul play are severely punished, and that their actions are not seen to be condoned. You cannot allow a game to continue with players who are determined to breach the letter and spirit of the game, as this ruins it for all the other players and may well lead to further problems as players decide to take the Law into their own hands.

When you have decided to caution or dismiss a player, the one important principle to remember is that you must stay in control. If you lose your temper, using bad language or violent gestures, you run the risk of further inflaming the situation and losing the respect of the players. Take your time: take the offending player(s) away from the others, walking backwards if necessary so that you can continue to watch what is going on. The captain(s) should come with you - it undoubtedly helps if he knows what is going on and what you're proposing to do. How you speak to the player(s) is a matter of personal preference, but make your point succinctly: 'You pushed a player illegally; if you use foul play again you'll be ordered from the field of play'; or 'Punching - off!' Make your decision and the reasons for it absolutely clear to the player(s) and the captain(s). You must show the player either a yellow or red card, but you are not expected to brandish it flamboyantly! The cards are a confirmation of your decision, and are not to be used to abrogate your responsibility to communicate.

You must note down a number of details in addition to the player's full name, team, position and number. You have to record the score at the time, the time of the offence, the half in which it took place, the distance you were from the incident and whether you had a clear or obstructed view of it. All these details are needed for the Disciplinary Body.

A further point here concerns the option of a general team warning. Law 26 authorises the referee to give a general warning after repeated infringements, but it also gives the referee the discretion to decide whether a series of offences by different players of the same team amounts to repeated infringement. If the referee decides that it does, then he can issue a general warning to the team and, if the offence is repeated, he must order the offending player from the field. Although this is a nice sanction to have, it should never be used. It can be enormously unfair, punishing a player who has done nothing wrong for the rest of the game. Caution players one by one and, if necessary, send them off. If there is persistent infringement, warn the captain that the next player will get a caution and the following player after that will be ordered from the field of play.

Of course, there will be times when you choose not to caution or dismiss a player but you still want to give him a good ticking-off. Follow the same procedures as above, taking him away from the other players before telling him why you are talking to him. A few well-chosen words of sensible advice can often prevent worse incidents occurring later in the game. Do not hesitate to take both captains to one side if you feel the players are not responding positively to you and your decisions: put the onus on them to get their players to conform with the Laws and respect your decisions and authority.

When you have touch judges appointed under Law 6, use them and look out for their signals on foul play. Consult them and, when they have signalled for foul play, ask them for all the necessary details and their recommendation for the penalty.

There is one aspect of foul play that perturbs referees, and that is the brawl. The first rule is not to get between the brawling players: nobody expects you to sort out two or more props having a go at each other! Blow your whistle loudly once, and get the captains to sort it out.

(8.4) Foul play - referee's checklist

When referees manage foul play effectively, the following elements are observed.

- Potential flash-points (e.g. pile-ups, collapsed scrums) are quickly dealt with.
- The game is managed in accordance with its temper.
- Touch judges are used effectively as extra pairs of eyes and ears.
- Referee's positioning allows him to see all aspects of the game, both on and off the ball.
- Offenders are swiftly and effectively penalised.

(9) Understanding the game

Referees are an integral part of the game of rugby. They are active and vital participants, and they are vested with significant authority and influence. Their decisions on the pitch, and their behaviour off it, both contribute to the general health of the game.

Refereeing is not, therefore, an adversarial skill. As a referee, you are not pitting your wits against the players, or trying to catch them out and prove your superior knowledge. You are there to help the players, to manage the game with due regard to equity, safety and the Laws. As a consequence, the good referee makes every effort to understand the game fully at all levels, and to offer players and coaches the benefit of his knowledge and experience so that the game progresses and improves. How do you do this?

The obvious place to start is at the club. The vast majority of referees are already club members, and have played the game at some level. The link between a referee and his club is a vital, but often under-utilised, channel of communication. You will probably know many of the players already, as well as the coaches and officials, so spend time with them and find out what they're thinking about the game, and how they play it. Join them for pre-season training, and watch the set-piece manoeuvres; offer your advice to the coaches, so that they know how referees are likely to interpret different situations. They may not want or accept your advice, but most are very happy to hear another informed point of view.

You can also get involved with mini- and youth rugby, where clubs are always keen to take on new coaches; if the senior players of the future are taught how to play the game within the Laws, you'll be doing an enormous service. Additionally, you should be another medium of communication for mid-season changes in Law or interpretation. Although clubs are always advised of such changes, the information doesn't always filter down to players and coaches as quickly as it should, and you can ensure that they do know what's happening - and why.

If you find yourself without a fixture on a Saturday afternoon, go and watch a game - or, better still, offer to run the line. You'll find that you have a completely different perspective as a referee. Many referees say that they have to record matches on television so that they can watch them twice: once to see what the referee does and once to enjoy the game. You will naturally find yourself watching the referee, and you should learn from what he does. But you should also take the opportunity to study the players and how they behave. When you're refereeing, there are many times when you come off at the end of a match and you have no idea of what kind of game it was and what the overall strategy of each team was. You've been so focussed on the micro-view that you haven't had a chance to appreciate the larger picture. Watching from the sidelines helps to develop that vision, and gives you a better understanding. And don't confine yourself to watching senior rugby. Go out on a Sunday morning and you'll find some very high quality colts fixtures played to the under-19 Law variations.

There are many other ways to enhance your perspective of the game. We all know that the media has a completely different view of rugby, and that they tend to be interested only in the big matches. Read the press reports of these games, and see if the referee is mentioned: if he isn't, it probably means he had a very good game! Watch rugby programmes on television and see how the commentators and summarisers deal with different issues: do they know and understand the Laws? In some cases they don't, but it's useful to hear what others think of referees and their decisions. As importantly, their analysis of coaching strategies and tactics can teach you a lot about how the game is being played, and what you should be looking out for.

Nowadays there are numerous videos available to help you learn from the experts. Top referees are wired for sound and you can listen to them as you watch the game. We can all learn something from watching the best in action, even if we never aspire to the same heights. They all started off at the bottom of the ladder and worked their way up by studying the winners and developing their own style. There is no better education than seeing a referee who is in complete control, calmly and effectively managing the game without being obtrusive. Apply the principles in this chapter and you'll be well on the way to achieving that state of grace!

CHAPTER 3

Continuity

Everyone enjoys a rugby match which flows well and where the ball is constantly recycled quickly and brought back into open play. Referees have a major part to play in facilitating this, and the way in which they manage situations undoubtedly has a significant influence on how the game develops.

Continuity is all about setting the right platform so that the ball continues to move and does not become static or trapped. Although it is primarily the responsibility of the players to achieve good continuity, the referee can help by using preventive and punitive measures.

The phases of play which fall under this heading are **Law 18 - tackle, lying with, on or near the ball; ruck and maul; advantage; and open play.**

(1) Law 18 - tackle, lying with, on or near the ball

Although Law 18 is a relatively short one, it is also very complex. Because of this, it is vital that the referee is always up with play and arrives at the breakdown quickly so that he can see exactly what is happening and can give preventive instructions to the players. Effective management of Law 18 is absolutely critical to ensuring continuity in the game: when it is refereed well there will be a free-flowing game; when it is not, the game becomes static.

Essentially, therefore, Law 18 deals with situations where the ball-carrier or the ball goes to ground, and the major underlying principle of the Law is that players can only participate if they are on their feet. Once they have gone to ground, they must take positive action to get up before they can play the ball or tackle other players.

(1.1) The tackle

According to the Law: ... *a tackle occurs when a player carrying the ball in the field of play is held by one or more opponents so that while he is so held he is brought to the ground or the ball comes into contact with the ground.* A player is not tackled if he is merely held and stays on his feet without releasing the ball.

There are three primary areas of focus for the referee at the point of tackle: the tackled player, the tackler(s), and the arriving player(s).

The **tackled player** has a number of options, which can be learnt by use of the acronym **PORAGOM.**

He must immediately ...

Pass the ball
Or
Release the ball
And
Get up
Or
Move away from the ball.

If there is one word in the Laws which causes more problems of interpretation than any other, it must surely be 'immediately'. Some referees work on the basis that the word contains five syllables and that the tackled player's action should take no longer than it takes to say the word. However, there are shades of interpretation that are dependent upon the circumstances. For instance, if the last man in defence is tackled near to his goal-line and has no support, and the tackler gets to his feet straight away, the ball release must be rapid. If, however, he is in midfield and is well supported, he may take slightly longer to place the ball as long as there is no unreasonable delay and his side are clearly in control.

Even if he releases the ball immediately, the tackled player must not simply lie on the ground and assume that there is no more to be done. He must make an effort to roll away or get up, unless it would be more dangerous to do this than to stay on the deck. The referee should encourage him by shouting: 'Move away!'. If he doesn't, and the referee thinks he could have, he must be penalised.

There are many situations which look inherently illegal but are, in fact, perfectly permissible. Law 18 allows the tackled player to release the ball, or place it, or push it along the ground, in any direction as long as it is not forward and the action is immediate.

This includes the situation where a tackled player falls so that he is facing the opposition goal-line; he is entitled to bring the ball over his body and push or throw it sideways or backwards towards his own goal-line. It looks terrible, but it's legal! What he is not allowed to do is roll over the ball so that he is then facing his goal-line.

The tackled player can also score a try, or make a touch-down on or behind his own goal-line, if he complies with the Laws: again, the emphasis here is on the immediacy of his action. He cannot be tackled in one movement and then initiate a separate movement to obtain the try or touch-down. His momentum must take him to or beyond the goal-line.

The **tackler** is also under an obligation to do something positive if he goes to ground in the making of the tackle. He must release the tackled player and get up or move away from the tackled player and the ball, and **he cannot play the ball until he is on his feet again**. Even when he is standing, the tackler cannot attempt to take the ball from the tackled player before he has released or passed it. If he gets in the way of opponents, interferes with play whilst on the ground, or prevents opponents from getting to the ball, he must be penalised. When the tackler moves out of the way, he enables the tackled player to comply with the Laws; the referee can help in this process by telling the tackler to 'Move away'.

In addition to these restrictions, referees should also pay attention to Law 26, Foul Play. Early, late and dangerous tackles - including the stiff-arm tackle and tackles above the line of the shoulders - are very serious infringements, and the referee is advised: *Players who wilfully resort to this type of foul play must be ordered from the field.* Similarly, a player who charges or knocks down the ball-carrier without any effort to grasp or hold him, or who tackles a player who is off the ground when fielding a kick, is guilty of dangerous play and must be punished severely.

At the tackle, **arriving players** must also comply with the basic principle of staying on their feet. These players must not go to ground and can only play the ball when they are on their feet. The only exception to this is when, following a tackle, the ball travels into the in-goal area: a player may then fall on the ball for a try or touch-down. The body position of arriving players will give the referee a good indication as to their intentions. Ideally, the players should be in a crouched position with straight backs and heads looking up. If they are rushing in with bent backs and heads down then they are likely to fall over, and can be penalised as they are making no effort to stay on their feet.

The referee can effectively manage the tackle situation with good communication. When the tackled player goes to ground and is still holding the ball, the referee should shout: 'Release!'. Both the tackled player and the tackler need to be reminded of their duty to move away - 'Get away!' - and the arriving players must be encouraged to conform with the Laws - 'Stay on your feet!'. Remember, too, that there is no offside in the tackle; as well as being good play, it is legal for the tackler to turn his opponent so that he is facing the wrong way or to approach him from what appears to be the wrong side.

(1.2) Lying with, on or near the ball

There are obviously circumstances in which a player who has not been tackled goes to ground in open play, the most obvious being when he is covering an opponent's kick ahead. Again, this player is under an obligation to do something positive, and the same acronym **PORAGOM** can be used as a reminder.

The player going to ground must immediately get up on his feet with the ball or ...

Pass the ball

Or

Release the ball

And

Get up

Or

Move away.

A player is not allowed to fall on or over the ball emerging from a scrummage or ruck (unless the ball is in the in-goal area).

What is critical here is the action of the next arriving player(s). They must remain on their feet and they must allow the grounded player to get to his feet or play the ball - a shout of 'Let him up!' is a good reminder for these players.

(1.3) Law 18 - referee's checklist

As mentioned, the referee's primary concern is to ensure that the game is played only by those players on their feet. When the ball or a player goes to ground, the referee has to manage the situation firmly and quickly: when he does not, there are likely to be pile-ups of bodies and unproductive, static ball.

Under Law 18, the referee will therefore:
• arrive at breakdowns quickly, and get into a position to manage the situation
• ensure that tackled players release and/or play the ball immediately
• ensure that tacklers are not allowed to interfere with the release of the ball
• keep arriving players on their feet
• prevent pile-ups, where bodies are on the ground and the ball is trapped, thus resulting in static play
• take preventive and punitive action.

(2) Ruck and maul

One of the major challenges for referees is to identify and manage rucks and mauls. Well-managed rucks and mauls result in an exciting game, whilst badly-managed ones create static rugby and offer significant opportunities for flash-points and dangerous play. Perhaps the biggest challenge for the referee in these situations is knowing where the ball is, and that can only be achieved by good positioning. Along with this, the referee has to remember what happened immediately prior to the ruck or maul forming because, if the ball subsequently becomes unplayable, this will affect the decision on which side gets the put-in at the resulting scrummage. Helpfully, the Laws give the referee guidance on this decision in those cases where he could not determine precisely who had control.

(2.1) Ruck

Law 21 defines a ruck as follows. *A ruck, which can only take place in the field of play, is formed when the ball is on the ground and one or more players from each team are on their feet and in physical contact, closing around the ball between them.*

This Law encourages the player in possession to get the ball on the deck and form a ruck as, if the ball subsequently becomes unplayable, the team moving forward prior to the stoppage will normally get the put-in at the resulting scrummage. This contrasts with the maul Law, which awards the scrummage the other way when the ball becomes unplayable.

Typically rucks are formed at a breakdown in play, i.e. after a tackle or when a player has gone to ground to recover a loose ball.

Remember that, according to the definition, players on the ground do not qualify as participants in a ruck: therefore, if the ball, the tackler and the tackled player are on the ground with no-one else there, it is not a ruck. Rucks can also be formed from mauls, where the ball is legally brought to the ground (as opposed to collapsing the maul, which is illegal).

Players advancing to the grounded ball should be permitted to take one step over the ball and any players lying near it. However, the practice known as 'scatter rucking', where players fan out and engage with opponents some distance from the ball, is illegal. Although handling in the ruck is not permitted - and is a penalty offence - it is acceptable for a player, such as the scrum-half, to recover the ball with his hands from the back of a ruck when it is obvious that his side has won control. Similarly, the hindmost player in the ruck can legally 'paddle' the ball backwards - this is an experimental variation on the Laws in England.

(2.2) Maul

According to the Laws: *A maul, which can only take place in the field of play, is formed by one or more players from each team on their feet and in physical contact closing round a player who is in possession of the ball.* This means that there must be **at least two players** from the side in possession of the ball **and an opponent** to constitute a maul. If the ball carrier is the only player from that team to be involved, opponents can come in from any direction to try and win the ball.

Coaches, players and referees all want the same things from a maul: they want it to be tidy, symmetrical and dynamic. When the maul is untidy - players wrestling for the ball, the maul lurching around or becoming static - there is little strategic advantage to be gained for either side, but most especially for the side in possession immediately prior to the start of the maul. When the ball becomes unplayable, the scrummage is awarded to the team not in possession at the beginning of the maul - so it makes sense for the side in possession to get the ball on the deck and create a ruck, to get the ball out of the maul as quickly as possible, or to keep the maul moving.

Commentators sometimes mistakenly refer to a rolling maul when, in fact, they mean a series of separate mauls, in which the side in possession breaks away and another maul ensues; but, if the maul becomes stationary, it cannot restart and the referee must stop play. However, in this situation the referee should allow a reasonable time for the ball to emerge but not allow the maul to start moving again. What constitutes 'reasonable'? A sensible interpretation is for the referee to shout, 'Use it, Blues', three times before he will blow. He must use some discretion if he can clearly see that one side has won the ball and that it is likely to emerge within that timescale.

One of the biggest problems for the referee with the maul is determining when it has been illegally collapsed - pulled down by the team not in possession as a destructive measure - and when it has been legally turned into a ruck by a player getting the ball on to the deck. It is illegal to collapse the maul, and the Law also says that, if the ball-carrier in a maul goes to ground and the ball is not immediately available for the continuation of play, a scrummage should be ordered. Players wrestling for the ball in a maul may try and bring the ball-carrier down as well, and this should be prevented by the referee. It is also illegal to attempt to drag opponents out of the maul; this is particularly common when players believe that opponents are in an offside position. If they are offside the referee should penalise them but, quite often, they are there legally because they have come into a tackle from the opponents' side. In this situation the referee should shout: 'He's there legally; leave him alone!'.

(2.3) Positioning at ruck and maul

To manage rucks and mauls effectively, the referee must get to the breakdown quickly in anticipation of a ruck or maul being formed, and he has two main priorities. He must determine the exact position of the ball, and he must encourage all participants to stay on their feet.

Clearly, in situations where a ruck or maul is formed as a result of a tackle, the referee will be particularly concerned about the safety of players on the ground, and he must be especially vigilant about use of the boot. There is a widely held misconception that it is a player's right to ruck these grounded people out of the way of the ball with their feet. Not only is this illegal, it is also highly dangerous; it is the referee's duty to look after those players and, wherever possible, to make them move away as quickly as possible.

Having moved in close to the ruck/maul to locate the ball, the referee should move away and take up a position where he can still see the ball but can also get a better all-round view of play (*see* **Figure 1**). In most cases this is best achieved by moving towards the side more likely to win the ball and facing the other side, at an

angle, so as to observe offside by both participants and non-participants. Don't be afraid to move all the way around the ruck/maul
in your effort to keep track of the ball, but be aware of where you
are standing so that you do not obstruct the players - and, once
you've located the ball, you don't need to keep on circling the
ruck/maul for the sake of it.

Figure 1 Positioning at ruck and maul

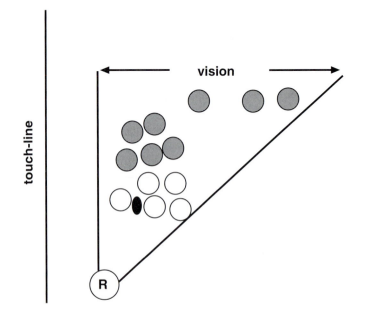

(2.4) Offside at ruck and maul

The offside line at rucks and mauls is defined as: *a line parallel to
the goal-line through the hindmost foot of the player's team in the
ruck or maul.*

Essentially, players must not join a ruck or maul from their opponents' side, or in front of the hindmost player of his team in the
ruck/maul (which means that they can join level with the hindmost player having come from behind the offside line).
Additionally, players who are not participating must retire behind
the offside line and stay there until the ruck/maul is finished.
Players who are in the ruck/maul and then unbind must also
retire behind the offside line (*see* **Figure 2**).

Figure 2 Offside at ruck and maul

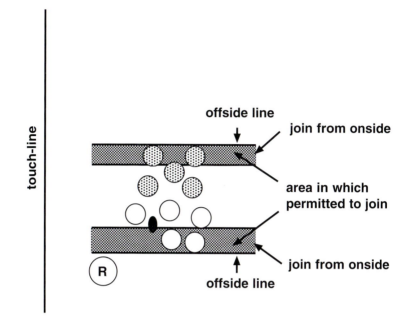

Referees should also pay attention to obstruction, or shielding. This occurs when a player at the back of a ruck/maul takes the ball and begins a new movement by backing into his own players rather than letting them join on to him from behind. If the ball-carrier is protected by a wall of his own players, they are obstructing the opposition and must be penalised.

Rucks and mauls which are formed at the line-out have a similar offside line, subject to the caveat that participants in the line-out do not have to join the ruck/maul but must observe the other off-side lines of the line-out. The referee needs to watch for two offences here, at the front and the back of a line-out.

Firstly, the participants at the back of a line-out may choose not to join the ruck/maul, but they must not leave the corridor of the line-out, especially when they drop away past the 15-metre line. If they move beyond that line, and the line-out is still in progress, they must retire 10 metres. Secondly, the opponent of the player throwing in the ball may decide not to join the ruck/maul, and they must not stray over the offside line of that ruck or maul.

(2.5) Major offences at ruck and maul

A player joining the ruck must have his head and shoulders no lower than his hips, and he must bind on with at least one arm around the body of a player of his own team who is in the ruck. This means that a player who is in a ruck, but who is not binding on his own players, is there illegally and should be penalised if he interferes with play.

The only way to get the ball out of a ruck is with the feet: use of the hands or legs is illegal (with the exception of the scrum-half or hindmost player as previously mentioned). Players on the ground must not interfere with the ball and must make every effort to roll away from it. It is also illegal to drag away an opponent who is lying on the ground in a ruck. Wilful collapsing of a ruck, and falling over or kneeling, are penalty kick offences.

Most major offences at the maul are the same as for the ruck, with the exception that a participant does not have to bind as long as he is caught in or bound to the maul by other players: if he is in this position he should be protected as other players may think he is offside. Say, 'He's OK', or blow quickly to prevent offences.

(2.6) Ruck and maul - referee's checklist

The key elements of successful ruck and maul management are as follows.

- Players remain on their feet, with wilful collapsing penalised.
- Players join level with or behind the hindmost player.
- Dangerous play - especially rucking of players lying on the ground - is severely dealt with.
- Offside by participants and non-participants is observed and prevented.
- Participants are correctly bound.
- Heads and shoulders are no lower than hips.
- Consistent application of 'reasonable time' to allow the ball to emerge from static mauls.
- Mauls which have become static are not allowed to start moving again.
- Obstruction/shielding is penalised.
- Handling in the ruck is penalised.

(3) Advantage

By now it will have become obvious that the referee has an enormous amount of discretion written into the 28 Laws. Of all the Laws, Law 8 (Advantage) gives the referee the most scope to exercise this discretion. A note to this Law even states: *The referee is given wide discretion as to what constitutes an advantage and is not limited to a territorial advantage. The referee is the sole judge of whether an advantage has been gained.*

In a typical game there are so many infringements that the referee could be blowing almost continuously. Although this might show a good knowledge of the Laws, it is not what the game of rugby is all about, and such a referee would be not be demonstrating any understanding of, or feeling for, the game. The players want to play, and they are dependent on the common sense of the referee to let them. The advantage Law is therefore a critical area.

Many advantage situations are clear-cut: a player knocks on accidentally, an opponent recovers the ball and gains territory as a result - no need to blow for the original infringement as the non-offending team has won a benefit. But players don't always realise that advantage is being played - and, somewhat surprisingly, they don't always appreciate it even if they do know. Take that last example: the non-offending team might prefer to have a scrummage in their favour, rather than let play continue, because they are dominant up front and would prefer a set-piece move from the scrum. Is it the referee's job to analyse and understand this? It probably isn't, although he must be sympathetic to the temper of the game and its structure. He also has to consider, above all else, the safety of the players, and advantage should not be played if he thinks that is in jeopardy.

So the referee needs to think not just about **territorial** advantage, but also **tactical** advantage. Say, for instance, that a penalty kick infringement is spotted by the referee inside the non-offending team's 22-metre area. He lets play continue because the defending team is in possession of the ball and has an opportunity to gain an advantage. The ball is kicked to touch in front of the place where the infringement occurred. Now the referee has to decide whether an advantage has actually been gained, because the mere opportunity is not sufficient. The offending team will have the throw-in. Is that fair, or should the non-offending team be awarded a penalty kick so that, if the kicker finds touch, his side will have the resulting throw-in? Note (vii) to Law 18 states: *Advantage shall be played only if it occurs immediately.* It is up to the referee to decide how to interpret that last word.

As a guide, unless a team has demonstrated a willingness to run the ball from any position, including behind their own goal-line, the referee will normally award a penalty immediately for any relevant offence which takes place within the non-offending team's 22-metre area.

There are few easy decisions about advantage, and each case has to be judged on its merits. If the referee has an empathy with the game, and knows the strengths and weaknesses of each side, he will be much better placed to decide on when to play advantage and when not. Above all, he must be consistent in his application of this Law for both sides.

The primary advantage signal - one arm outstretched at waist height in the direction of the non-offending team - is not particularly well known by players or spectators. It is very helpful for the referee to shout, 'Advantage to Reds', as he outstretches his arm: the players then know that you've seen the infringement and are trying to let the game flow. For penalty kick offences, good referees will tell the non-offending side that they have seen the infringement, and that they will penalise the offending team if no advantage is subsequently gained. It also helps to remind the players to play to the whistle, rather than to stop as soon as they've spotted what they think is an infringement.

But for how long should you allow the non-offending team to try and gain an advantage? Is it three seconds, five seconds, or even longer? Again, this depends on the nature of the game, and can only be decided when you're on the pitch and in the middle of the action. You will know if advantage should be applied; you will have a good idea of whether the non-offending team has any chance of gaining from their opponents' infringements; and you will be able to judge whether the players appreciate a longer or shorter advantage period. Use your common sense: should referees play advantage, for instance, when the ball has become static - especially in Law 18 situations - and there is a well organised defence? Don't play advantage for the sake of it.

One small, but important point to bear in mind: don't get fixated by exactly where the original offence occurred. Keep up with play when you're applying advantage; if you need to bring play back you can be sure that, wherever you make your mark for the scrummage, free kick or penalty kick, the players won't know any better than you.

Advantage is therefore strongly linked to your understanding of the game, and your appreciation of what the players are trying to achieve. How you read the game will affect your decisions regarding advantage.

There are three restrictions on the use of advantage by the referee, and neither team may gain an advantage from the following.

- When the ball or a player carrying it touches the referee.
- When the ball emerges from either end of a scrummage tunnel.
- When there is an irregularity in play that is not provided for in the Laws (e.g. a dog runs on to the pitch and bites a player!).

There's one other point to remember: the referee has to strike the right balance between playing advantage and ensuring that players conform to the Laws through his use of appropriate sanctions. Especially in the first 10 minutes of a game, referees are setting out their stall, conditioning the players so that they know what to expect if they infringe. A good understanding of the game, however, may allow you to play advantage from the very first whistle, providing you let all the players know you are in control.

(3.1) Advantage - referee's checklist

- Advantage is played giving due consideration to the temper of the game and the safety of the players.
- Advantage is applied consistently.
- Recognition that, in many cases, the penalty kick is the major advantage, especially in defensive positions.
- Consistent verbal and hand communication that advantage is being played, and that advantage had been played.

(4) Open play

The term 'open play' covers a multitude of situations and is mainly concerned with what happens before or after a scrummage, line-out, restart kick, tackle, ruck or maul.

In open play, the referee has to be positioned well to spot infringements and, wherever possible, to prevent them through clear and concise instructions. Players, coaches, spectators and referees share a desire to see a good, open game in which both sides can play to their full potential; the referee is pivotal in ensuring that this happens through his positioning, skill, discretion and judgement. Being in the right place, and having a global view of the game, are vital to achieve this.

(4.1) Positioning in open play

New referees often have a major problem in knowing where to be for any particular situation, especially if they have taken up the whistle after a long career as a player. Running lines for referees are completely different from those for players, and a good referee rarely stands still: he is constantly looking for the optimal position to see the ball and the majority of the players. If he is too close to the action, he runs the risk of missing infringements and, in the worst case, obstructing players.

There are three elements which help the referee to keep up with play:

• his angles of running
• his change of pace
• his awareness.

(4.1.1) Angles of running

Wherever possible, the referee needs to take the direct route to follow play. The direct route does not always mean the shortest route: short cuts can cause serious problems. For example, the ball comes out of a scrummage and the scrum-half goes down the blind-side, with you standing on the open-side. The short cut might be to come round the back of the scrum of the opposing side, anticipating that you will get in front of play on the blind side. But, in doing this, you are immediately blocked by the defending back row as they break off and you are unable to see what the blind-side flanker and winger are doing to defend against the scrum-half's action.

A better route would be to follow the scrum-half around his own side of the scrummage, even though this means you are behind play. With this positioning, you will at least have a better chance to see infringements and to monitor the defending players' actions. Following the passage of the ball and the ball-carrier is therefore key.

Angles of running for the referee are all about diagonals. Remember how you should position yourself at set-pieces, slightly angled to the play so that you can see both the ball and the majority of the players. Running lines follow the same principle, so that you are working almost diagonally to the passage of play. You need to be able to see forward passes, knock-ons, offsides, and dangerous play, and you need to be able to look behind you to see what's going on as the set-piece breaks up. A diagonal running line helps you to achieve all this. Bear in mind, too, that you will be watching your touch judges for their signals.

Figure 3 Angles of running

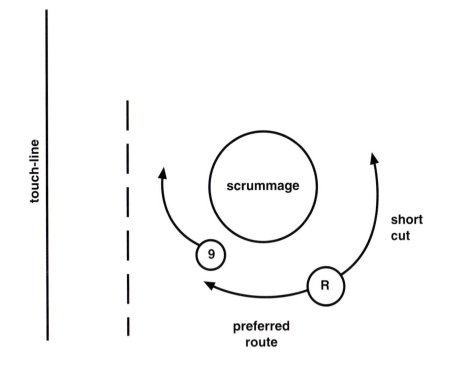

(4.1.2) Change of pace

At set pieces, such as a scrummage or line-out, be on your toes and ready to move off quickly, rapidly changing up 'through the gears' so as to keep up with play as soon as the ball emerges. This, of course, can only happen if you are fit and have worked on your acceleration and sprinting: you must have that initial burst of energy to enable you to get to the ball quickly without the effort resulting in a loss of concentration.

(4.1.3) Awareness

The good referee will also use his awareness to make reasoned predictions on the choices available to players in open play. Are they most likely to kick, to pass, or to run? Which way will they go? You cannot always accurately anticipate where play will go, but you do need to be aware of the most likely options so that, whichever one is taken, it will not surprise you and leave you flat-footed and out of position.

(4.1.4) Near the goal-line

Nowhere is good positioning more critical than near the goal-line. Events which take place in or near the in-goal area are crucial to the result of the game and, more than anywhere else on the field, the referee will be expected by the players to get it right here and to communicate decisions clearly, quickly and confidently.

First of all, you have to be very clear about what the in-goal area is: *In-goal is the area bounded by a goal-line, touch-in-goal-lines and dead-ball line. It includes the goal-line and goal posts but excludes touch-in-goal-lines and dead-ball line.* This means that a touch-down or try can be made on the goal-line, or against a goal post.

For the referee, there are several factors to bear in mind when play is near the in-goal area.

- He must be aware of where the goal-line is and cross it in advance of play wherever possible, **except** at a moving maul where he should keep the ball in view.
- He must be a little in front of play and, if necessary, be prepared to take short cuts from a ruck, maul or set-piece in order to see the ball being grounded.
- He must get as close as possible to the point of touch-down without getting in the way.
- He must be prepared for the unexpected (remembering that a drop-goal may be attempted and he needs to be well positioned for it).
- He must take careful note of who last played the ball before it goes into the in-goal area, because this will determine the restart after the ball is dead if no other offence occurs.
- He must remember that, for most offences in-goal, the penalty is the same as for a similar offence within the field of play (except that tackle, ruck, maul, scrummage and line-out can only take place in the field of play).

If there is any doubt about whether the ball has been grounded on or beyond the goal-line, the referee should award a 5-metre scrummage to the attacking team. Near the goal-line is also the area where the penalty try is most often awarded. A penalty try, which is awarded under the posts, is given in a situation where, but for foul play by the defending team, a try would **probably** have been scored, or it would **probably** have been scored in a more favourable position (i.e. nearer the posts) than that where the ball was grounded. Don't forget that, if you award a try and you are abused by the defending players, you are within your rights to award a penalty kick to the opposition as the restart from the half-way line.

Positioning in open play is therefore a combination of factors.

- Following the passage of the ball and ball-carrier (in preference to taking a short cut).
- Gaining sight lines not blocked by other players, and avoiding blind spots.
- A preference for in-field positions rather than touch-side.
- Close attention to play on or near the goal-line.
- Avoiding looking directly at the sun.
- Anticipation of the flow of the game - through a tactical appreciation - to ensure you stay in a good position.

(4.2) Offside in open play

Offside is one of the most important components of refereeing open play. The Law states that a player is offside in open play when in front of a team-mate who has the ball or last played the ball. A player who is offside in this way is out of the game until put onside again, and must not take any further part in the game or move towards opponents waiting to play the ball.

How is a player put onside? There are four ways in which he can be put onside by his own team.

- The team-mate, with the ball, runs past and in front of him.
- The team-mate behind, who has kicked the ball, runs past and in front of him.
- Any other team-mate, who was onside when the ball was kicked, runs past and in front of him.
- The offside player runs back behind onside team-mates.

Figure 4   Onside by own team

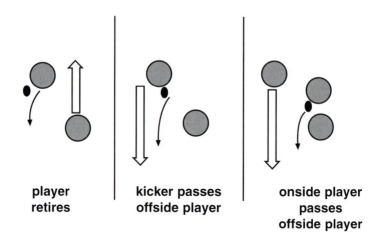

player **retires**	**kicker passes** **offside player**	**onside player** **passes** **offside player**

If the ball is kicked, and an offside player is within 10 metres of the opponent waiting to catch the ball, he must move out of the 10-metre area or be penalised, because he cannot be put onside by any of his own players. A quick shout of 'Retire!' when the ball is kicked forward will remind offside players of this obligation.

Figure 5 Offside: 10-metre zone

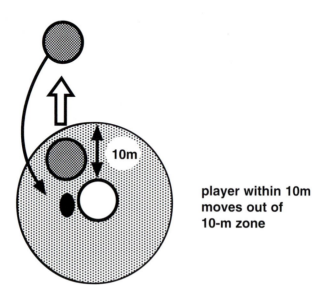

player within 10m moves out of 10-m zone

Opponents can put an offside player onside in three ways:

• by running 5 metres with the ball
• by kicking or passing the ball
• by intentionally touching, but not holding, the ball.

The important thing to remember about offside in open play is that there is no penalty for the offence unless the offside player does something negative, like obstructing an opponent or moving towards the opponents waiting to play the ball. You should also differentiate between deliberate and accidental offside, and you should, wherever possible, allow the non-offending team to try and gain an advantage.

The penalty for deliberate offside is a penalty kick where the player was first offside or, at the option of the non-offending team, a scrummage at the place where the ball was last played by the offending team. In the situation where more than one offside player move towards the opponents, or to the place where the ball pitches, the mark for the penalty will be that of the offside player closest to the player waiting for the ball or where the ball pitches.

(4.3) Open play - referee's checklist

You should be concentrating on the following elements in open play.

• Management of offside, especially from kicks ahead, looking at the 10-metre exclusion zone, forward movement, and players in front of the kicker.
• Obstruction in open play, including shielding of players and crossing (where a player walks in front of a team-mate carrying the ball to protect him from a tackle).
• Positioning for play near the goal-line.
• Positioning to see knock-ons and forward passes.
• Positioning for dropped goals.

CHAPTER 4

Restarts

For the purist, restarts from the scrummage and line-out remain the most fascinating part of the game. Seeing the packs in a close physical contest is exciting and these set-pieces, when properly managed, are one of the highlights of rugby.

For the referee, there are several challenges in managing restarts - **scrummage, line-out, kick-off, drop-kick, penalty and free kicks.** Above all, the way in which a referee manages the situation just before a restart is critical to whether this phase of play is successful or not. Preventive refereeing is the key - stop players from infringing before a restart and you are much more likely to exercise the necessary control and to avoid flash-points.

(1) The scrummage

The scrummage is one of the classic set-pieces of rugby. It is also, from the referee's perspective, one of the most difficult to manage. There are numerous possible areas for infringement, not only by the participants but also by the backs. It is probably fair to say that the scrummage presents the referee with his most challenging tasks as regards safety of players: there are significant potential dangers for front rows that are badly set or mismatched, and the referee will ensure that all possible steps are taken to avoid injury to the players.

The scrummage Laws (Law 20) are specifically designed with safety in mind, and the referee needs to pay particular attention to all aspects and to abide by the letter of the Laws in this area. A well managed scrummage is an absolute prerequisite for a good game, as it is the most frequently used method of restarting the game after an infringement. For the scrummage to be managed well, the referee needs to establish his standards from the start; in fact, this is an area that he should consider telling the players about before they go out on to the pitch. If you tell the front rows in advance exactly what your setting procedure will be, there is less scope for misunderstanding once the game has begun.

Scrummages normally result from what can be described as non-destructive infringements - accidental knock-ons, forward passes, static mauls, trapped ball in the ruck, for example - and are awarded to the non-offending side or otherwise according to the Laws. The game is restarted at the mark where the infringement occurred, unless the Laws allow for alternatives (e.g. so that the feet of all participants remain in play, line-out infringements where the mark is on the 15-metre line, illegal drop-outs and restart kicks, infringements in the in-goal area). The referee signals the nature of the infringement, the award of a scrummage and the side which has the put-in. He also makes a mark with his boot to show the central line of the scrummage, around which the two packs should set themselves.

Typically there are four different kinds of scrummage, and you may - if you're very unlucky - encounter all of them in the same match.

- Positive.
- Negative.
- Passive.
- Destructive.

(1.1) The positive scrummage

In the positive scrummage the dominant pack will set itself correctly, with shoulders parallel to the ground and all eight participants facing directly forward. They will shove in a straight line and push their opposition backwards without trying to disrupt the scrum through any illegal manoeuvres. You are most likely to see an example of a positive scrummage when there is a put-in for the attacking team on the 5-metre line or close to the goal-line. Your primary concern in this situation is to ensure that the opposing participants are safe and are not infringing and, when near the goal-line, to position yourself so that you can clearly see when and if the ball reaches the goal-line. This is because the scrummage ends once it is on or over the goal-line and, of course, there is likely to be a touch-down in this scenario.

(1.2) The negative scrummage

Players, coaches and referees often refer to 'the secrets of the front-row union'. Even if you have been a front-row player yourself, it is very difficult as a referee to spot all the actual infringements which occur in this area, however much you may suspect illegal actions. However, there are various signs which tell you that one or both front rows are engaged in negative scrummaging, and various ways of preventing it.

Much of the negative activity can be obviated by proper setting of the front rows. The recommended sequence for engagement of the front rows is: **crouch, pause, engage**. The Law confirms this: *Before commencing engagement each front row must be in a crouched position with heads and shoulders no lower than their hips and so that they are within one arm's length of the opponents' shoulders. In the interests of safety, each front row should engage in the sequence of crouch, then pause and only engage on the call 'Engage' given by the referee.* (In under-19 rugby, this sequence is extended so that it becomes: **crouch, touch, pause, engage**.)

Negative scrummaging starts when one or both front rows decide to hinder this process. A front row may be in the crouch position but does not line up heads and shoulders at the same level and angle. This makes it much more difficult for their opponents to engage against them. Additionally, the hooker may obstruct the tight-head prop by moving his head so that the prop cannot put his head in the space between the hooker and his loose-head prop.

By getting the front rows to set and engage precisely as the Law demands, there is much less opportunity for negative scrummaging, and the referee needs to get this right from the first scrummage. It is therefore quite acceptable to tell the skippers before the game exactly how you intend to set the scrums, and what sequence of commands you will use. Some referees will say, 'When you're ready,' to indicate that the front rows can engage; others will go through the entire setting sequence. What's important is that both front rows know what you're going to do and say, and that you follow this consistently for the whole game.

(1.3) The passive scrummage

There will be passages in the game where both packs decide that they will simply lean into the scrummage without applying any major force. This can occur after prolonged periods of open play, when one or both packs are very tired, or when the scrummage takes place in midfield and there is no particular danger or potential advantage from the position. Problems may occur here if one pack then decides to put on a shove, in which case the passive pack will be caught off guard and may well collapse, or resort to negative or destructive tactics to prevent it.

(1.4) The destructive scrummage

Even if you manage to set the scrummage well, you still face significant potential problems if one or both packs - especially the front rows - decide to employ destructive tactics to hinder an effective and legal process.

There are two relevant Laws here.

Law 20 states: *Players in the front rows must not at any time during the scrummage wilfully adopt a position, or take any action, by twisting or lowering the body or by pulling on an opponent's dress, which is likely to cause the scrummage to collapse.*

Law 26 (Foul Play) states: *It is illegal for any player:*

- *in the front row of a scrummage to form down some distance from the opponents and rush against them*
- *in the front row of a scrummage wilfully to lift an opponent off his feet or force him upwards out of the scrummage*
- *wilfully to cause a scrummage, ruck or maul to collapse.*

It should be noted that the penalties for Law 26 infringements are severe; the referee is instructed either to order the offending player off or to caution him that he will be ordered off if he repeats the offence. This is obviously in addition to the award of a penalty or penalty try.

You can tell a good deal about participants' intentions by looking at their body positions and, as importantly, the placing of their feet and the angle of their legs. If the shoulders are above, or level with, the hips, the thighs vertical, and the knees bent at the angle needed to maintain this position, a forward shove is effectively produced, and there is less likely to be a problem in the front row (*see* **Figure 6**). When any or all of these positions are not in evidence, this is a signal that destructive tactics may be under consideration. The challenge for referees is to spot who is infringing; in some cases a front row player may be innocent but is forced into a poor position by the actions of his opponent.

Figure 6 Body positions of front row

Note the change of angle whilst the thigh remains vertical.

Possibly the easiest infringement to spot is **pulling down**. This occurs when a prop (usually the tight-head) binds to his opponent with his outside arm so that he is exerting a downward pressure. It is easy to spot because, with his arm bent, his elbow will either be pointing towards the ground or upwards. However, some very strong props will still be able to exert a downward pressure with the elbow straight: in this case the forearm will be pointing downwards. Pulling down is a penalty offence, as it is extremely dangerous and destructive. The outside arms of the props must be as level as possible, and it is the referee's duty to keep the elbows up and the wrists level. Ideally, a prop's forearm should be parallel to the ground.

The tight-head prop may also engage so that his body position is driving towards the shoulder and head of the opposing prop - the manoeuvre known as **boring**. This again is a penalty offence. To spot this, the referee should take a position which allows him to see over the top of the set scrummage; from this angle he can check whether the tight-head props are in a position for 'an effective forward shove'. Clearly, it is preferable if the referee takes preventive measures, asking the props to straighten up if it appears that they are not set properly.

Collapsing the scrummage can be caused by other methods apart from pulling down and boring. These include pulling the leg of a prop, either by the opposing prop or flanker - this offence is very serious and warrants at least a caution for the offending player. Be alert to the binding of the loose-head prop, who may get under the opposing tight-head and pull down. A hooker can also collapse the scrummage by getting his head lower than his hips and driving downwards with his back bent. These actions are normally accompanied by a change of angle at the knee - the knee is driven forward so that the thigh ceases to be vertical (*see* **Figure 7**). Collapsing the scrummage is obviously a very dangerous manoeuvre and must be penalised - again, preventive action can be taken by the referee so that all the players are set for the forward shove and comply with the legal body positions.

Figure 7 Change of front row body position

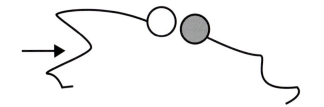

Another dangerous scrummage offence occurs when one pack dips slightly once the ball is in the scrum and then rises, shoving upwards instead of forwards and getting underneath the opposing front row so that it is unable to stay crouched and its bindings break. Once the engagement has been broken the scrummage is at an end, but that may not stop the offending team from continuing to push. The 'dip and pick' manoeuvre is legal, however, as long as the resulting drive is straight ahead rather than upwards.

Bear in mind that **wheeling** the scrummage is not an offence, even though it may cause problems. The scrummage must not wheel more than 90 degrees from its original position: when it does, the scrummage is reformed and the put-in goes to the side who had gained possession or otherwise by the same team.

Although the majority of destructive tactics in the scrummage are employed by the front row, you must also pay attention to the back row. The flankers are allowed to bind at any angle to the pack, but they are not allowed to change their position once the ball has been put in. This Law stops them from swinging out to obstruct the opposing scrum half as he follows the ball round to the back of the scrum. Additionally, the flankers are not allowed to bind on opposing players with their outer arms, which is a free kick infringement.

The referee must also check that the back rows stay bound until the scrummage is over. Law 20, (6), (d) states: *All players in a scrummage, other than those in a front row, must bind with at least one arm and hand around the body of another player of the same team.* This means that the whole arm, from wrist to shoulder, must be bound. Back row players can put their heads up as long as they stay bound. The number eight can also bind in three different positions at the back (*see* **Figure 8**); there is no obligation in Law for him to put his head between the locks. Again, a few well chosen words - 'Stay bound' - will help to keep the back row legal.

(1.5) Scrummage management

To achieve control of the scrummage, the referee needs to be alert to all the potential problems listed above - and one of the best ways of managing the scrummage is to be in the right place. Positioning at the scrummage is particularly important because the referee also needs to have a clear view of the backs. The challenge for the referee is to know where to stand to get the broadest possible view so that he can watch the actions of the packs and still be properly positioned to see whether the backs are encroaching beyond the onside line.

Figure 8 Binding of number eight

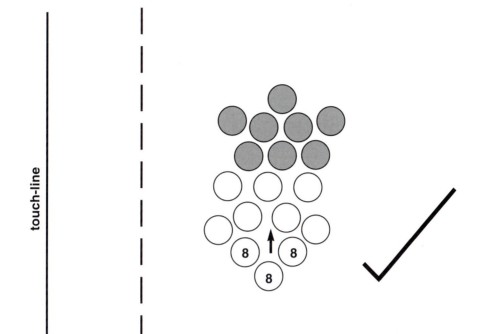

When setting the front rows before they have engaged, the referee will normally stand at the side of the scrummage from which the ball will be put in (and remember that there is no restriction on which side is used). Do not stand directly between the front rows; they don't like this as they want to look at the opponents and see where they are going to engage - and you are liable to be caught in the middle when they do engage. Instead, stand close by the side and hold one or both arms outstretched into the space between the front rows. When they are crouched and you give your signal - 'Engage', or 'When you're ready', for example - you take away your arm to give them a further signal that they can engage.

At this point you must move away quickly so that the scrum-half has access to the tunnel. Pull away to the side and turn so that you are almost facing the team which does not have the put-in, but do not step back too much because you want to be watching the tunnel for a crooked feed and foot-up. At the first few scrummages you may want to remind the scrum-half that he is obliged to put in the ball without delay - 'Straight in, scrum-half' - so that he knows what you want. Delaying the put-in is a free kick offence; it is normally the hooker who signals the timing of the put-in and, if he is delaying his signal, then make sure you have a word to get him to speed up the process. Once you are satisfied that the ball has gone in straight, you should stay in your original position for just a few moments to check on the behaviour of the front rows.

If there appear to be problems on the other side of the scrummage, ask the scrum-half to hold the ball until you've got round there to identify what those problems are. You can always set the scrummage from 'the wrong side' if the need arises. Remember that the good referee is a manager and a problem-solver, so go to where the problem is and get the players to take responsibility for implementing your solution to the problem.

You should follow the ball as it moves to the back of the pack which has won the ball, far enough away from the side of the scrummage so that both scrum-halves can move around without interference (*see* **Figure 9**). You need to be here to watch the flanker to see if his body position changes to obstruct the opposing scrum-half, and you're also well positioned to check on the backs for off-side. Additionally, you need to be alert to back row players unbinding before the scrummage is over.

Figure 9 Positioning of referee during scrummage

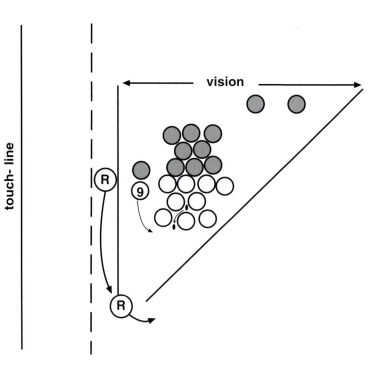

Keep on checking the front rows for destructive actions and, as the ball reaches the back of the scrum, begin to move towards mid-field, making sure that you do not limit the options of the number eight and the scrum-half by standing in an obstructive position. With this in mind, you may choose to stand on the 'wrong' side of the scrummage if it is very close to the touch-line; this will then allow the scrum-half to kick for touch without having to get the ball past you, and it will position you better if he passes it to a receiving player for an attempted drop-goal.

From **Figure 9** you can see that the recommended movement and positioning of the referee allow him a clear path to the next phase of play without obstructing the players, and that he can see both the scrummage and the backs.

Be aware of the effect that field position may have on subsequent play. Look at the three scrummage positions in **Figure 10** and con-sider how play is most likely to develop for the attacking side after a successful scrummage.

Figure 10 Tactical options at scrummage

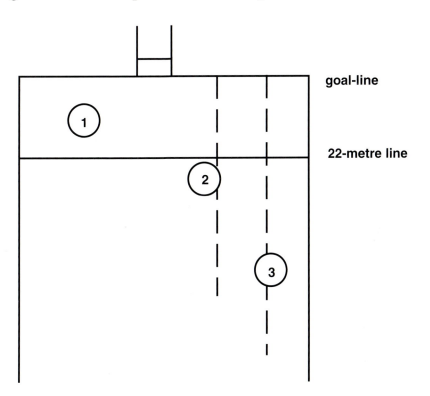

At scrummage 1, what is the most likely option the attacking team will take:
• push over?
• number eight drive for the line?
• crash ball at centre?

Are these options more likely than:
• miss-out pass to outside centre, with full-back in the line?
• miss-out pass to outside centre, miss-out pass beyond full-back to wing?

If this is the range of possibilities, think about where you would next want to be, to be close to the action.

At scrummage 2, what is the most likely next point of attack:
• blind through 8, 9 and 11?
• open through 8, releasing to 6 to run at defending 10 and 12?
• open through centre field?

If this is in descending order of likelihood, where would you like to be when the next action develops?

And, at scrummage 3, what's more likely:
• box kick by 9?
• pass to 10, bomb to defending 15?
• back row infield, ruck/maul/release outside backs?

Again, by making some prejudgement (which could be wrong, but more often than not is likely to be right), you can anticipate the next point of action, and be there.

Don't stop refereeing the scrummage as soon as the ball is out. The scrummage is a potential flash-point and front row players may have more interest in resolving private battles than in getting to the next break-down. Many infringements occur when the referee's back is turned, so be vigilant of the scrummage break up. Here it obviously helps if you have a touch judge.

(1.6) Offside at the scrummage

There are three offside lines at the scrummage: two lines parallel to the goal-lines through the hindmost foot of the players in the scrummage, and the line through the position of the ball (*see* **Figure 11**). The two 'hindmost foot' lines are for the backs to observe: they cannot move up beyond that line whilst the scrummage is in progress. The 'ball' line is for the scrum-half whose side has not won the ball: as he moves round the scrummage to follow the ball back he must not place either foot in front of the ball. This player must also stay in 'close proximity' to the scrummage; this means that, if he moves away from the scrummage to adopt a defensive position, he must retire behind the 'hindmost foot' offside line.

Figure 11 Offside lines at scrummage

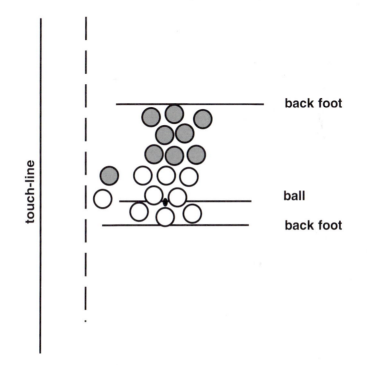

back foot

ball

back foot

touch-line

(1.7) Scrummage - referee's checklist

To recap, here are the referee's key priorities for effective management of the scrummage.

- He follows the correct engagement procedures: front row bodies parallel to the touch-line; front row in pushing position; heads straight; binding correct; scrummage stationary; head and shoulders above hips.
- He interferes minimally if the scrummage is stable and working.
- He manages the collapsed scrum.
- The ball is put in immediately, straight and at the correct distance.

- He observes offside by participants, including back rows remaining bound until the scrummage is over.
- He observes offside by non-participants.

Additionally, the referee should do the following.

- Set the scrummage in the correct position and place.
- Ensure the scrum-half is 1 metre from the scrum.
- Prevent the opposing scrum-half from touching the scrum.
- Prevent flankers from swinging out.
- Take preventive action.
- Take punitive action by penalising.
- Position himself to achieve all of the above.

Note Remember that the Laws for under-19 rugby vary quite significantly for the scrummage, both in terms of managing the engagement and in the way the participating players form the scrummage. There are also variations on wheeling, the distance the scrummage can move with the ball in, as well as restrictions on the scrum-halves at under-15 level.

(2) The line-out

Before looking at the line-out - and the quick throw-in - we need to consider the issue of the ball in touch.

(2.1) Touch

According to Law 23 (Touch and Line-out), the ball is in touch:

- when it is not being carried by a player and it touches a touch-line or the ground or a person or object on or beyond it.
- when it is carried by a player and it or the player carrying it touches a touch-line or the ground beyond it.

It's important to understand these definitions, because there are circumstances in which the ball can cross the plane of the touch-line but not be in touch. For example, if the ball is kicked to touch and it crosses the plane of the touch-line and then recrosses back into the field of play, without having landed or touched anything beyond the touch-line, the ball did not go into touch. A more obscure example is when a player is tackled and, whilst still holding the ball, he ends up on top of the tackling player: if neither the ball-carrier nor the ball makes contact with the touch-line, or the ground beyond it, the ball is not in touch and he can pass or release it so that it goes back into the playing area and play continues.

Additionally, a player with both feet in the playing area can catch, deflect or tap the ball, even when it has crossed the plane of the touch-line, and keep the ball in play as long as both his feet remain in the playing area.

With touch judges, the referee's job in making decisions about touch is substantially easier. Without them, the referee must apply common sense - and, as mentioned earlier, he will already have made it clear to the teams that he is not there to run the line.

(2.2) Quick throw-in

The simple fact that the ball has gone into touch does not mean that a line-out will follow. Subject to certain restrictions, the side throwing in the ball can choose to take a quick throw-in, and the referee must be alert to this.

A quick throw-in is permissible under the following conditions.

• The ball that went into touch must be used, and it must only have been touched by the player throwing it in (so it cannot be given to him by another player or spectator), except that, where a player has been forced into touch with the ball in his possession, a quick throw-in by the opposition is allowed.

• The line-out must not have formed (a formed line-out consisting of at least two players from each team lining up in single lines parallel to the line of touch).

• The throw-in must be from any point along the touch-line between where the ball went into touch and the goal-line of the team throwing in the ball.

The touch judge will keep his flag raised, but will not put out his other arm in a horizontal position, if he adjudges that a quick throw-in is permissible.

For the quick throw-in to be valid, the ball must travel at least 5 metres straight along the line of touch before it hits the ground or is touched by another player; if it doesn't, then the opposing team has the choice of throwing in the ball or taking a scrummage on the 15-metre line. If a player prevents it from going 5 metres, it is a free kick to the non-offending team.

Figure 12   Quick throw-in - allowable area

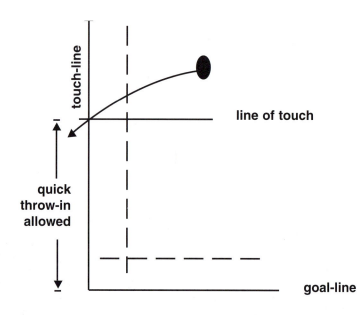

Figure 13   No quick throw-in allowed

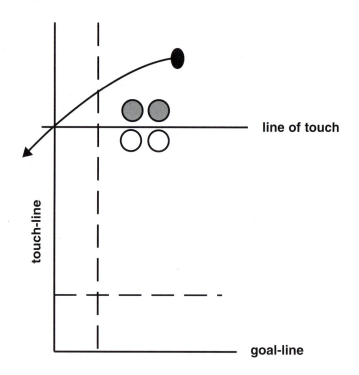

(2.3) Award of the throw-in

Normally the ball is thrown in by an opponent of the player whom it last touched, or by whom it was being carried before being in touch. The exception to this is the penalty kick: when the ball is kicked directly into touch from a penalty kick, the ball will be thrown in by the team which kicked the ball into touch.

The line of touch is an imaginary line across the field of play which runs at right angles to the touch-line through the place where the ball went into touch (or, in the case of a quick throw-in, where the ball is thrown in).

The line of touch is determined as follows.

• From a penalty kick, or from a kick within 22 metres of the kicker's goal-line (including a free kick awarded within that area): at the place where it touched or crossed the touch-line.

• From a kick directly into touch other than as specified above, or when the kicker receives the ball outside his 22-metre line and retreats behind the line before kicking it or throws, knocks or kicks the ball back behind the line and retrieves it himself and kicks it: opposite the place from which the ball was kicked or at the place where it went into touch if that place is closer to the kicker's goal-line.

There are special Laws concerning drop-outs, kick-offs and restart kicks.

• If the ball is kicked directly into touch from a kick-off/restart, and the opposing team elects to accept the kick, the line-out is formed at the half-way line or where the ball went into touch, if that place is nearer to the kicker's goal-line.

• If the ball is kicked directly into touch from a drop-out, and the opposing team elects to accept the kick, the line-out is formed where the ball went into touch.

(2.4) Formation of the line-out

Although a line-out has to be formed by at least two players from each side, there is no maximum. Theoretically, the side awarded the throw-in can choose to have 14 players in the line-out, as long as they are all within the zone between the 5- and 15-metre lines. The side throwing in determines the maximum number of players from either team who can participate; the opposition can have less, but not more, players. When shortened line-outs are called, it's a good idea to shout, 'Numbers', for the opposition. As the referee, you don't want to be standing there counting the participants while the ball is thrown in and, by doing this, you put the onus on the non-throwing side to line up properly. Be pragmatic about this: if players are genuinely making an effort to retire to the onside line when the line-out is shortened, don't automatically penalise them if the ball is thrown in whilst they are still offside, as long as they continue to retire and do not rejoin the line-out.

The two lines form on either side of the line of touch. The players must stand on their side half a metre from the line of touch, so that there is a 1 metre gap between the two lines (measured from shoulder to shoulder). This is a minimum and maximum measurement. The line-out stretches between the two lines - at 5 and 15 metres - which run parallel to the touch-line from which the ball is being thrown in.

Figure 14   Line-out

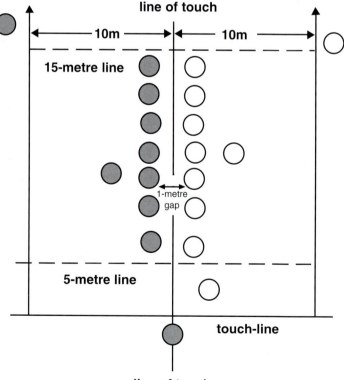

The participants in the line-out are the two lines, the thrower and his immediate opponent, and the two players acting as scrum-half. Every other player is not participating at the line-out and must observe the Laws which govern them (*see* section 3.5).

Without touch judges, the referee has to monitor the formation of the line-out and ensure that there is a 1-metre gap and that the two lines are straight, i.e. parallel to the line of touch. To do this, the referee should stand on the line of touch at the front of the line-out as it is forming. The 1-metre gap is absolutely critical, because it gives the jumpers enough space to jump for the ball without infringement. Space at the line-out has to be the referee's major concern, so set the lines well. Enlist the help of the first men in each line - normally props - so that they know where you want them to stand. They can then hold their hands up to mark the line for their colleagues.

Most referees agree that walking along the gap is not a good idea: as likely as not the hooker will throw in the ball whilst you're standing in the middle and you'll be in big trouble. Referees should step to one side once they are satisfied that the line-out is properly formed (and *see* section 2.7 on positioning).

(2.5) Offside at line-out

There are six offside lines at the line-out.

- The line of touch.
- The ball.
- The 5-metre line.
- The 15-metre line.
- 10 metres from the line of touch, parallel to the goal-lines, on either side of the line-out.

Participants are not allowed to cross the line of touch, unless they do so in the act of jumping for the ball and have started from their own side of the line of touch. They cannot take up a position in front of the ball unless they are carrying it or have tackled, or attempted to tackle, the ball carrier and they started the tackle from their side of the ball. They are not allowed to move beyond the 15-metre line until the ball has been released by the thrower, and then only if they are anticipating a long throw-in. The Law here is very specific: *If players so move and the ball is not thrown to or beyond them they must be penalised for offside.*

ılk about an imaginary corridor in which the line-out
ɛ. This corridor extends slightly beyond the outside
ɔf each line, between the 5- and 15-metre lines, and is
which the line-out takes place. The reason for this cor-
ɪɪuɔɪ is to accommodate the 'peeling-off' manoeuvre, where one or
more players move towards their own goal-line in anticipation of
catching the ball when it has been passed or tapped back by one of
their players in the line-out. Peeling-off is legal once the ball has
left the hands of the player throwing it in. The corridor also allows
players to move round behind their own line, once the ball has
been thrown in, to form a maul. Within the corridor, and subject to
the Laws' conditions, players can move without being offside.

Non-participants in the line-out have to stay behind the 10-metre
offside line until the line-out has ended. Defining the end of a line-
out is easy in theory, but difficult in practice.

> The Law says that the line-out ends when one of the
> following has happened.
>
> • A ruck or maul is taking place and all feet of players in the ruck
>   or maul have moved beyond the line of touch.
> • A player carrying the ball leaves the line-out.
> • The ball has been passed, knocked back or kicked from the line-out.
> • The ball is thrown beyond a position 15 metres from the touch-line.
> • The ball becomes unplayable.

What tends to happen is that, as soon as the ball is thrown in, the
defending backs move up, wrongly assuming that their offside line
has moved to the back foot of an ensuing ruck or maul. To stop this
happening, it's a good idea to tell both stand-offs what you want
them to do, and for them to act as your marker. If you have touch
judges, then the touch judge on the far touch-line will take up a
position on the offside line for the backs so that they can line up
with him. But, if you don't have touch judges, you'll have to monitor this, so you need to enlist the help of the stand-offs. You
should also be alert to the 'banana' line, where the stand-off and
inside centre are onside, but the outside centre, wing and even full-
back may encroach. It helps the players if you tell them your reading of the situation: 'It's not over, stay back!'. This isn't coaching;
it's simply preventive refereeing.

(2.6) Offences at the line-out

There are so many offences at the line-out that a whole book could
probably be written on this single subject. The temptation for the

referee is to decide that he will only concentrate on the most serious ones, and that those which do not interfere with play should be ignored. To an extent this attitude is permissible - other than for incidences of foul or dangerous play - because the Laws have been framed to encourage the ball to be recycled from the line-out as quickly as possible. If the ball comes away quickly and cleanly, and the 20-metre zone between the opposing backs is maintained, there is much more chance of an open, exciting game.

However, it is not the duty of the referee to encourage an open, exciting game at all costs. He has to make decisions and judgements about the nature of the infringements and the fairness with which the ball is won. If one side is consistently winning clean line-out ball, and moving it away quickly, you must consider why this is happening. Is it because of their technical superiority, or is it because they are deliberately impeding their opponents and stopping them from fair competition for the ball? If you don't look at this, you'll find 15 very angry players on the pitch.

As with most other aspects of the game, the Laws differentiate between what might be described as constructive and destructive infringements. For the participants, these are separated into across-the-line and along-the-line offences. The former take priority because they are likely to be destructive.

Across-the-line offences, which normally result in a penalty kick, occur when both sides of the line-out are involved. These include:
- offside
- using an opponent as a support when jumping for the ball
- holding, pushing, charging, obstructing or grasping an opponent not holding the ball.

Along-the-line offences, which normally result in a free kick, are related to only one side of the line-out. They include:
- peeling off and moving too far away from the line-out
- using another player of the same team as support when jumping for the ball
- lifting a player of the same team
- supporting any player of his own team before that player has jumped for the ball
- supporting a player of his own team below the waist (which is a penalty kick offence)
- standing within 5 metres of the touch-line or more than 15 metres from the touch-line until the ball has gone beyond them
- using the outside arm to play the ball, unless both hands are above the head
- closing the 1-metre gap, except when jumping for the ball.

Remember, too, that the non-participants can offend at the line-out by encroaching within the 10-metre offside line.

(2.7) Positioning at the line-out

Where should the referee stand at a line-out? There is no one answer to this question. Some like to stand right at the front where they can see the gap and can make sure that the space for jumpers is protected. Others change their position for every line-out, especially once they're satisfied that the gap is being maintained and they can look for other offences. A few, especially vertically challenged referees, prefer to go to the back of the line-out and watch for across-the-line infringements.

Figure 15   Positioning at the line-out

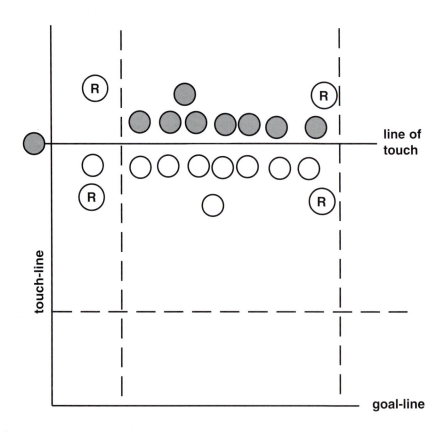

Because there are so many possible infringements at the line-out, the referee needs to decide what is important before he chooses his positioning. The gap must be set and maintained, so the referee needs to be close to the front of the line-out as it is forming. On a related point, the referee should be the first to the mark: it shows he is fit and keen and, more practically, he needs to be there in case there is a quick throw-in. As the line-out forms he is setting the standards; not only does he get the lines straight and properly separated, but he can also show the stand-offs where he judges their offside lines to be.

The line-out is also one of the few times when the referee can have a quiet word with players when the ball is out of play, and the opportunity should not be overlooked. 'Blue 6, I saw you offside at that last maul; don't do it again'; 'Scrum-half, put the ball into the next scrum quicker, will you?'. You have so few chances to let them know what you want, so take all of them. If necessary, tell the hooker not to throw in the ball until you're ready.

Never turn your back on the player throwing in the ball. You may think that you're still preparing the line-out, but he may think differently and release the ball before you're ready. If your back is turned, you won't be able to see if the throw is straight, or if it goes 5 metres, or if there is interference from his opposite number. Walk backwards away from him, and keep your body position angled so that you can see him, the line-out and the non-participants.

Early in the game you will probably want to stand at the front of the line-out. This enables you to see what's going on at the critical front positions: are the props obstructing each other?; illegally lifting their jumpers?; closing the gap?; or indulging in one of the many other tricks they can play? Are the jumpers staying on their marks or are they crossing the line? If possible, you should look into the eyes of these players so that they know you're watching them: you'd be amazed how their behaviour changes for the better if they know they're under scrutiny! Standing at the front of the line-out establishes your presence, even though it means you have to run further, and faster, when the ball gets out to the backs and into open play. Always stay on your toes so that you can move quickly to where the action is.

You should also avoid ball-watching: concentrate your vision on an area below the ball so that you are focussed on the likely contact areas between shoulder and hip. Some referees suggest that you should keep your chin on your chest to force yourself to look downwards: you can tell a lot about the intentions of the players by where their feet are and where they go. Of course you need to watch for the ball being thrown in straight, but you can judge that by the angle at which the jumper goes up to receive the ball. Do be alert to the fact that many subsequent infringements in the line-out - especially those across the line - occur as a result of a crooked throw, and that is the first offence.

If you decide to stand next to the jumpers, make sure that you do not get in the way of the scrum-half. Scrum-halves will not thank you for this and will waste no time in telling you if they think you're in the way.

Figure 16   Following the ball at the line-out

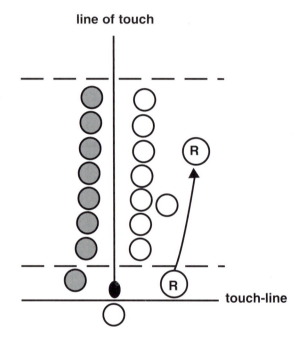

Standing at the back of the line-out has some distinct advantages. You can see the ball as it is thrown in, watch for across-the-line offences, and are well positioned both for a long throw and to monitor the backs. But this position does have its limitations, and it removes you from the immediate action which is more usually in the middle or towards the front of the line-out. It also separates you from the participants, giving them the impression that you don't care, or don't understand, what they get up to. If you want to go to the back, you should probably wait until you are completely satisfied that all is well in the line-out - or if you suspect that numbers six and seven are infringing. Once at the back, you must be very careful not to impede a long throw-in, and you've got to be sure that you'll be able to see a short throw-in to the front player in the line-out. If you have a touch judge, standing at the back is much less of a problem.

Finally, it is a general rule of thumb that you should stand on the throwing team's side of the line-out - but this is a rule which has many exceptions. The reason for standing on the thrower's side is that you assume his team will win the ball, and you will want to set your lines of sight and running so that, when it is won, you can follow play along the backs without having to run through a crowd of players. But you must be pragmatic about your positioning, not only because the ball is frequently won by the opposition. You may want to watch a particular player whom you suspect of infringement; you may have witnessed early domination by one side; and, most importantly, you must always stand on the goal-line side of a line-out when it is near to that goal-line. Why?

Firstly, you want to be ready for a participant to catch the ball and make a break for the goal-line, and you need to be in front of him to judge whether he grounds the ball for a try. Secondly, you are in a position which enables you to prevent offences by the defending

Figure 17   Positioning at line-out near goal-line

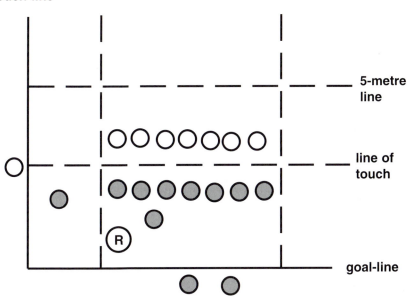

touch-line

5-metre line

line of touch

goal-line

side, such as offside by the backs. Thirdly, you can also spot infringements by the attacking team, such as the forward tap-through, where the jumper knocks the ball ahead of him for someone else to ground; the front peel, where a participant peels away and goes round illegally to the defending team's side of the line-out; and where the defending team's hooker is obstructed by the attacking player who has thrown in the ball.

(2.8) Line-out - referee's checklist

When the line-out is refereed well, the following elements will have been observed.

- Offences across the line-out are made a priority and are prevented and/or penalised.
- Offside by participants and non-participants is monitored.
- The ball is thrown in from the correct mark and along the line of touch.
- The quick throw-in is properly managed.
- The 1-metre gap is set and maintained.
- Lifting (as opposed to legal supporting) and illegal use of the outside arm are prevented.
- Participants remain within the 'corridor'.
- Preventive and punitive action is taken to achieve the above.
- The referee is always correctly positioned.

(3) Penalty and free kicks, kick-offs and drop-outs

One of the early lessons you will learn as a referee is the phrase: 'Never stop refereeing'. What this means is that, even after a stoppage, you should still be on your toes and looking around you, as plenty of incidents occur when the ball is dead and all appears calm. This is especially true at situations when play is restarted by a kick.

(3.1) Penalty and free kicks

For penalty and free kicks, the kicker's team have to behind the **ball** until it is kicked - most players think that they have to be behind the **kicker**, a misconception which is helpful to you as they tend not to infringe. The opponents must be 10 metres back from the mark (rather than the kicker, if he chooses to take the kick from behind the mark), and they are not allowed to enter the game until they have retired 10 metres, or until one of their team-mates who was 10 metres has run past and in front of them. At a free kick, opponents can charge as soon as the kicker begins his run or has offered to kick; if, in so doing, the opponents prevent the kick being taken, it is void and a scrummage is awarded to the opposing team at the mark.

Figure 18   Positioning at penalty/free kick

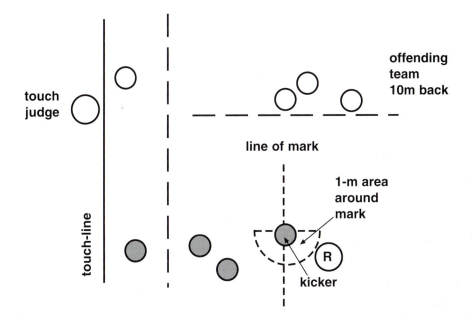

Tap penalties and free kicks can cause several problems for referees. You don't want to deny the kicking team an opportunity to gain an advantage so you must make the mark quickly and get away from it immediately so that they can take the kick in their own time, and you must give them some latitude as to exactly the spot from which they take it - a 1-metre area around the mark is reasonable. However, you have to mindful of the fact that the kicker may be looking for an unfair advantage by taking the kick quickly and running directly into opponents who have not retired. The opponents should not be penalised in this situation, but they must not interfere with play until they have retired the 10 metres or when one of their own players who was 10 metres back has passed them.

Some referees have decided to deal with this pragmatically, and will actually propose the following course of action to both skippers before kick-off: the referee will give the kicking team the first 10 metres if opponents do not retire quickly enough, but he will be slower in making the mark for the next kick so as to give the opponents more time to retire. The Laws appear to support this, saying that a further penalty or free kick should not be awarded if the referee is satisfied that the reason for this has been contrived by the kicker's team.

If a team says that it intends to take a kick at goal, that intention is irrevocable and the kicker cannot then change his mind. However, if he places the ball for a kick at goal and it then falls over, he can pick it up and drop a goal. For free kicks, and scrummages taken in lieu of free kicks, remember that a dropped goal cannot be scored until after the ball next becomes dead, or the ball has been played or touched by an opponent, or an opponent has tackled the ball carrier, or a maul has formed.

Where you stand for a penalty or free kick depends on the circumstances, but is usually as indicated in **Figure 18**. Once you have made your mark, you must move off in a lateral direction as quickly as possible, watching the opponents to make sure they are 10 metres back or are making an effort to retire. You will know whether the kicker is going to go for touch, take a tap kick, go for goal, or put up a high ball, so move into a position from which you can clearly see the outcome as well as watching most of the players. Keep on your toes at all times, ready to follow up all kicks regardless of the anticipated outcome: many kicks don't reach touch, for instance, and you've got to be prepared for that.

(3.2) Kick-offs

A kick-off occurs at the beginning of each half (when it must be a place kick) and after a score (when it must be a drop-kick). The kicker's team must be behind the ball **when kicked**: as with penalty and free kicks, most players don't realise this and think they have to be behind the kicker. The receiving team has to be on or behind their 10-metre line; if they aren't, the kick is taken again. A fair catch (mark) cannot be made directly from a kick-off. If the ball is kicked directly over the opposing team's goal-line, without touching or being touched by another player, and that team touches it down or makes it dead or it goes dead, they have the option of a scrummage at the centre of the half-way line or having the other team kick off again.

The referee needs to take up a position which enables him to watch the kicker's team as it moves up with the kicker, and to see the opposition (*see* **Figure 19**). He should be running as the kick is taken, but he must be careful to ensure that he does not get in the way if the kicker decides to change the angle of his kick. The referee also needs to be mindful of obstruction by the receivers: it's a common ploy for the catcher to be surrounded by team-mates, some or all of whom will form a wall in front of him, which makes them offside. Watch the catcher to make sure he isn't tackled in mid-air, which is dangerous play and should be severely dealt with.

Figure 19   Positioning at kick-off

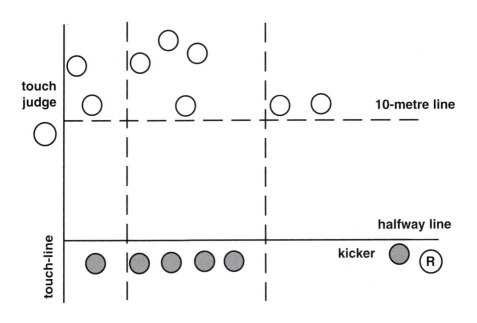

(3.3) Drop-outs

Drop-outs are fairly straightforward, but there are a couple of problems of which you should be aware. The kicker's team has to be behind the ball when kicked; if not, a scrummage is given to the non-offending team in the centre of the 22-metre line, but infringing players should not be penalised if their failure to retire is because of the speed with which the kick is taken. In these circumstances the offside players must not stop retiring and must not enter the game until they have been put onside by the action of their team-mates (*see* section 3.1 for details).

As long as the ball crosses the 22, play can continue, even if it is blown back or curls to such an extent that it comes back. Advantage can be played when the drop-kick does not reach the 22. If the attacking team makes the ball dead by a kick, other than an unsuccessful kick at goal, the defending team has the option of a drop-out or a scrummage; if they choose the latter, it will be ordered at the place from where the ball was kicked. This Law is designed to discourage negative kicking tactics.

The referee should stand on or near the 22 for the kick, and should be positioned so that he can see the majority of the players, but he must not get in the way of the kicker if he changes the angle of the kick. The referee should be running as the kick is taken.

Figure 20   Positioning at drop-out

(3.4) Restarts from kicks - referee's checklist

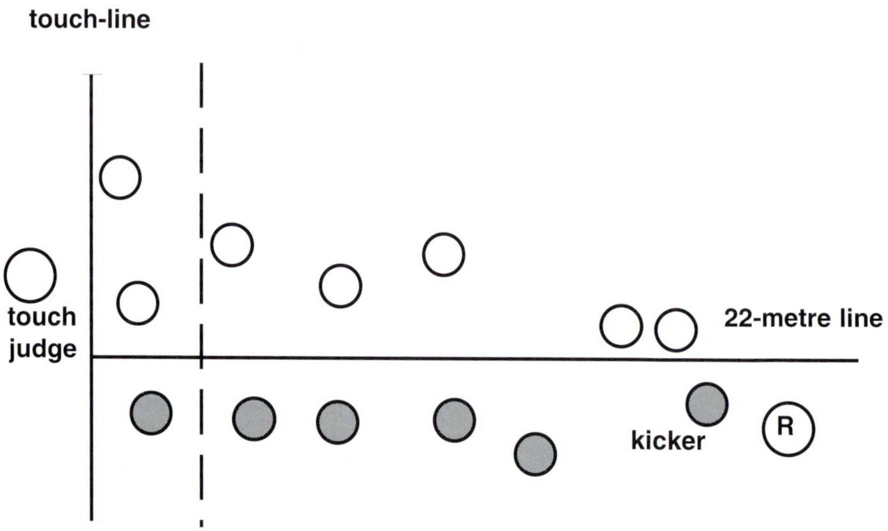

touch-line

touch judge

22-metre line

kicker

(R)

Essentially, there are two key points to observe for effective management of these restarts.

- Players must be behind the ball at kick-offs. They must be behind the ball at penalty and free kicks and drop-outs unless their failure to retire is due to the speed at which these kicks are taken and they must still conform to the offside Laws covering this situation.

- Management of penalty and free kicks - taken from correct place, referee moves away from mark quickly, kick correctly taken, 10 metres observed and enforced, ball made available by offending team.

CHAPTER 5

Getting on

As with any role that involves a high degree of responsibility, the task of refereeing goes hand-in-hand with training and development. It is in everyone's interests that all referees, at whatever level they operate, are properly prepared and, from the moment you pick up the whistle, you will be supported with a wide variety of training courses and materials, as well as more informal development media.

But that preparation is not a unilateral commitment. Successful referees are more than willing to participate in training and development programmes, and make a commitment to keep themselves informed about the game and the changing nature of the Laws and their interpretation. It is not sufficient simply to go on an introductory training course: referee development is a continuous process which never ends. As the game evolves, the Laws have to change to deal with new ways of playing, and referees need to know and understand how to adapt their management skills to handle new situations.

The Referee Society

The central point for most training and development is normally the Referee Society. These Societies are autonomous bodies, separate from the Rugby Football Union. They exist primarily to allocate referees to fixtures in their chosen geographic region: clubs in that region usually pay a membership fee to their local Society, in return for which they will receive referees for their games. The Societies are largely dependent on their member clubs to provide a continuing supply of new referees because, at the end of every season, a number of referees retire, move away or can no longer devote enough time. Societies and their member clubs work closely to recruit new referees, supplementing projects run centrally by the RFU like National Referee Week, a recruitment campaign which launched 'Willie Whistle', the referees' mascot. As these Societies have grown they have taken on a number of other functions, the most important of which is referee training.

Many Societies have appointed a Training Officer to handle this specific issue. There are basically two forms of training: formal programmes, developed centrally by the RFU, and less formal, but equally vital, meetings and discussion groups.

Foundation training

Formal training is based on the core **Referee Awards** - Level I for mini- and midi-rugby (under-7 to under-12), and Level II for under-19 rugby. These award schemes are designed as a comprehensive introduction to refereeing, and many Societies promote them as the base level of training for new referees. The award programmes are not intended as a substitute for learning the Laws, but focus on interpretation and game management. Society Training Officers run the award schemes, which tend to be over a number of evenings and culminate in a practical session where the attendees watch a game and comment on the referee's performance. Once referees have attended the course, they referee a certain number of games before receiving a certificate.

Not everybody, however, can make the necessary commitment to joining a Society and refereeing in various different locations every week. Recognising this, the RFU and the Referee Societies have developed the **Club Referee Certificate.** This course is specifically designed for people who want to referee but would prefer to handle fixtures at their own club. There is an increasing recognition that clubs can no longer pull 'old Fred' out of the bar just before kick-off, give him a whistle and hope he can last for 80 minutes. Nowadays all games, at whatever level, need to be managed by a qualified referee. Societies therefore encourage those who want to referee at their own club and support them with the Club Referee Certificate. However, it should be stressed that this certificate is merely the start of the training process, and it must be supple-mented with additional learning. Some Societies rightly suggest that participants in the Club Referee Certificate also join the local Referee Society so that they can benefit from ongoing training and development programmes and stay in touch with other referees.

A similar course has been put in place for teachers. The **Teacher's Referee Certificate** is aimed at those who want to referee under-19 games and is a one-day course which covers both theory and practice. It is vital that teachers are properly trained in the basic elements of refereeing. The Law variations for under-19 rugby put a heavy emphasis on safety, and the Teacher's Certificate reflects this. As with all other formal training programmes, this certificate provides a core of knowledge and understanding, but cannot be viewed as the complete training solution.

As you progress up the ladder, further training courses are available, where more emphasis is put on the finer points of refereeing - such as mental preparation, fitness, game preparation, and self-analysis. At the higher levels, referees are constantly monitored and are streamed according to competence and potential. Training and development is therefore a continuum, with performance benchmarks being raised as the referee progresses.

There are programmes at every level for referees who wish to climb the ladder. A **National Foundation** programme exists for those who start with a Society and want to referee adult rugby. As referees move into the C grades there is a national C grade programme which has to be completed before moving on to the B grade programme. For all of these the RFU has produced Tutor Guides, presentation packages and participant materials.

As referees progress above the B grade level, they move into the elite **RFU Panel of National Referees**, where training and development is focused on personal development plans which analyse individual refereeing goals, strengths, weaknesses, opportunities for development and threats to that development. This analysis culminates in an action plan. A sample action plan is set out below: it's never too early to start!

B1 Personal refereeing development plan

The purpose of this file is to provide you with an opportunity to generate your own refereeing development plan.

This should be seen as something to live with you so that you can monitor your progress and review your plans accordingly.

You can use it as a basis for discussion with a referee coach or mentor. You can keep your assessment reports in it. It is yours to keep and use as you require.

Personal refereeing goals

Outline below your refereeing goals/ambitions
including target dates.

-
-
-
-
-

Strengths

Record below your refereeing strengths.

-
-
-
-
-

Weaknesses

Record below the areas of your refereeing requiring
further development.

-
-
-
-
-

Opportunities

What opportunities are there for you to build on your strengths and
develop the areas requiring attention?

-
-
-
-
-

Threats

What are the threats to you achieving your goals, i.e. what is
hindering your progress?

-
-
-
-
-

Action planning
You
What actions can you take to build upon the opportunities and to minimise the threats?
-
-
-
-
-

Others
What practical actions can others take to help you to achieve your goals - who and what?
-
-
-
-
-

Mentor
Who are you going to discuss the personal refereeing plan with?

What qualifies them for the role of mentor:
- an elder statesman?
- another referee?
- a sports coach?
- a work place coach?
- a good listener?
- a confidant?
- a facilitator?

Clubs
Clubs train and/or plan at the same mental or physical pace at least four times a week. If you were to make the next steps which clubs could you visit to ensure that you are operating at that same pace?
-
-
-
-
-

When will you start working with them?

Within the RFU Panel of National Referees there are development squads which meet for training and development sessions. The top referees in the National Referee Development squad will have coaches whose task is to maintain the referees' performance at peak levels and help these referees to resolve any problems they may have.

The Training and Development pyramid is shown in **Figure 21.**

Figure 21   Referee development in England

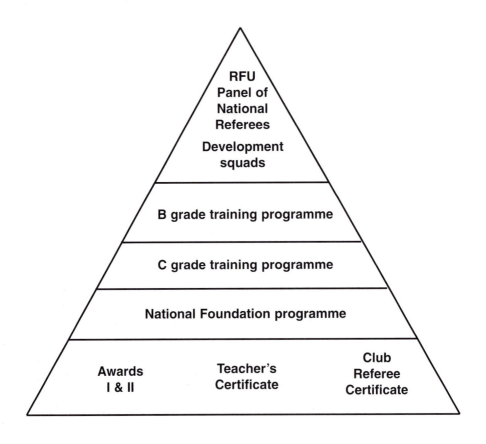

Society training

Although the Referee Societies are run by unpaid volunteers, that does not mean that their approach to the job is anything less than professional. Societies provide referees to all levels of the game and must therefore ensure that the training they give is comprehensive and tailored to specific needs. Typically, a Society will run monthly meetings - open to all - which will include administrative items on the agenda but which will be largely devoted to aspects of the game. For instance, a schedule of meetings might cover Law changes, the scrummage, onside/offside, communication, ruck and maul, the team of three and the line-out. These more informal sessions give the Societies and their referees the opportunity to discuss and debate issues which directly and indirectly affect them in a relaxed and friendly forum.

Society meetings also give referees a rare opportunity to meet each other in a social setting. There is enormous benefit in being able to talk to other referees, finding out how they handle particular situations and sharing knowledge and experience. Especially for new referees, these meetings are a valuable addition to the formal training programmes on offer.

Climbing the ladder

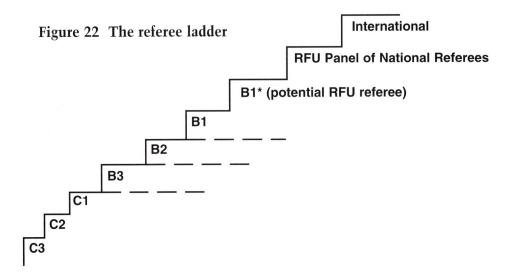

Figure 22 The referee ladder

For the new referee, the development process begins with foundation training - the Referee Awards, Teacher's and Club Referee Certificates. For various reasons, some referees do not progress beyond these awards, but there is no problem with this. They hone their skills working with children or the players at their own clubs. New Society referees are now expected to complete at least one of these courses, or the National Foundation programme, early on in their career, at which point they are graded as a C3 referee - the first rung on the ladder. The ladder then progresses as shown in **Figure 22.**

At each level the games start to change in standard, from junior clubs' third XVs to teams at level 5 in the leagues for B1 or B1* referees. The RFU Panel of National Referees rise to the dizzy heights of the First Division. To get there is a process which ensures that referees know how they are performing and how they can improve.

How am I doing?

Refereeing involves a significant investment of time and effort, and no-one wants to see that investment wasted. For any referee to improve - and, as importantly, to feel that they are improving - there has to be a method of assessment in place which accurately and objectively measures performance and potential. Most referees are naturally self-critical animals, and are much more interested in what they're doing wrong than in what they're doing right. They appreciate informed opinion, advice and counsel so that they can better themselves, as well as managing and enjoying their games more.

Referee performance measurement, of course, can never be entirely scientific. Both the assessor and the assessed are only human, and no measurement system can legislate for personal foibles and idiosyncrasies. However, the RFU, the clubs and the Referee Societies have developed a number of different ways of looking at the performance of referees which, when taken as a whole, give an excellent indication of existing skills and weaknesses and areas for future development.

Club grading cards

Clubs have to be happy with the referees provided to them. This does not mean to say that referees set this as a top priority, but it is obviously important that the clubs value and respect the work done by referees and their Societies. Without that level of trust and confidence, the game would soon collapse. As a result, clubs are often asked to assess the performance of their referees for each fixture.

Societies provide referees or clubs with grading cards which are handed to both captains before the game. These cards ask the captains (or Club Advisers) a variety of questions about the way in which the game was managed by the referee, and the captains or Club Advisers are expected to give a mark for each element of competence. Individually the scores cannot be used as a completely valid method of assessment, but over the course of a season there will undoubtedly be discernible trends. No referee can hope for absolute consistency of grades, because the scores awarded by captains will vary according to their knowledge of the Laws, their position on the field, the result of the game and numerous other factors. However, club grading cards are very important for three reasons.

•They demonstrate to the clubs that the referee administrators are keen to improve the quality of refereeing, and value the opinion of the clubs they serve.

•They deliver important data on the players' perspective of a referee's performance - after all, if the players aren't happy, something is obviously going wrong and needs to be addressed.

•They are the primary method of referee assessment at the lower end of the game.

Societies encourage clubs to fill in and return the cards as part of the post-match routine. The results are fed into a database which is then used as one element in the performance measurement process. Referees receive their individual results on a regular basis and can use these to concentrate on aspects of their performance which need further development.

The club cards are simply one strand in the assessment process, and no referee's career is dependent solely on the input of the clubs. The grades represent a trend, and a view from one constituency of the game. If weaknesses are highlighted by these grades, there are more formal and objective methods of remedial action.

The Competence-based Referee Development System

Whilst input from clubs is important, referees also need to be monitored more formally - and the best people to perform that task are other referees! Only when you have been a referee can you know how difficult and challenging the task can be, and you have a much greater empathy with the referee as a result.

The RFU has devised the Competence-based Referee Development System to inject higher levels of consistency into the process of performance measurement. The system is based on Units of Competence, which cover all the major elements of a game - Management of the Game, Management of Touch Judges, Scrummage, Line-Out, Law 18 (Tackle), Ruck and Maul, Advantage, Open Play, Communication, Fitness, and Positioning. Each Unit of Competence is scored according to a pre-determined set of criteria.

Very good - to be awarded when all the elements of competence are covered consistently throughout the game.
Good - awarded when all the prioritised elements of competence are covered consistently throughout the game.
Minor development - awarded when, on most occasions, the prioritised elements of competence are adhered to.
Needs development - awarded when there is clear evidence he has knowledge of and has adhered to all elements of competence but has not applied them consistently throughout the game.
Significant development - awarded when the referee has demonstrated a knowledge of the elements of competence but has not adhered to them effectively nor consistently.

Additionally, the Adviser provides information on the referee's potential, indicating what needs to be done to fulfil that potential.

Referee Advisers, drawn from the ranks of existing and retired referees, use the system to assess the performance of referees and, more importantly, to provide feedback and advice to both the individual referee and his Society. A standard form is used by the Adviser (*see* pages 96-7), with copies being provided to the referee and his Society.

The Referee Adviser normally introduces himself to the referee well before the game and then gets out of his way! He observes the referee's pre-match preparations and the way in which he interacts with the players and club officials; he may, if invited, also attend the touch judge briefing from the referee (if touch judges have been appointed). One of the special skills of the Adviser is to understand that he is not there to watch the game: his sole interest is the referee's performance and his management skills. He will not make any comments at half-time or other breaks in play: this is important because the players get used to thc particular style of the referee during the game and this should not be disrupted.

After the game, when the referee is showered and changed, the Adviser will give his feedback on the referee's performance. This is intended to be a constructive and informal session in which the Adviser highlights the important areas that need attention - and gives praise where it is due! This session also gives the referee an opportunity to seek advice and clarification on any aspect of his game, so it should be a conversation rather than a lecture.

Once the report has been completed by the Adviser and received by the referee and his Society, it will form another part of the performance measurement analysis. Assessments by Advisers become

RUGBY FOOTBALL UNION   **REFEREE REPORT FORM**

Name of Referee_____Grade_____Society_____

Match Type   _____Level_____Date   _____

Match   _____(pts) -v- _____(pts)

1.   **Description of the Game :**

2.   **The Referee's Management of the Game :**

Please assess the Referee's Management of the Game using Criteria :

3.   **The Referee's Management of Touch Judges :**

4.   **The Referee's Potential :**

Please assess the Referee's Potential using the Criteria :

Signature of Adviser :   **Date :**

Name :   **Society :**
(Please use block capitals)

5. **Units and Elements of Competence**

Please assess the Elements of Competence for each unit using VG, G, MD, ND, or SD, adding comments to explain any criteria below Very Good. It may be appropriate to provide praise when something has been done very well i.e. a VG.

Scrummage	
Lineout	
Law 18	
Ruck & Maul	
Advantage	
Open Play	
Communication	
Fitness	
Positioning	

For RFU appointments please return this form to the Referee Department at Twickenham.
For all other appointments please return to the Adviser Administrator as notified by your group or society.

more frequent as you move up the ladder and are handling more important fixtures, although most Societies aim to have all their referees assessed on a regular basis. The system has resulted in significantly higher levels of consistency and objectivity, to the benefit of all concerned.

The mentor (minder) system

There are never enough Referee Advisers to cover as many fixtures as would be ideal, so some Referee Societies have introduced mentoring as a supplementary method of helping referee development.

A mentor is someone who, through his experience, is in a position to help others develop their potential.

This help comes in four ways:

- as an **adviser** to help clarify what needs to be achieved and possible routes for development
- as a **coach** to help develop a realistic view of skill levels and how to improve them
- as a **facilitator** to help identify or create appropriate opportunities for development
- as a **counsellor** to assist the referee in solving his own problems.

Particularly at the beginning of your career as a referee, you are likely to run into some problems, both in terms of your performance on the pitch and the administration and management of the game off the pitch. It isn't always easy to find the answers to all your questions, so some Societies have put a mentoring system in place so that referees have someone to whom they turn when they need information or clarification.

Although no two Societies operate the system in precisely the same way, the principles are fairly similar. Experienced referees act as mentors: they are likely to have a group of referees of different grades under their wing, some of whom will need more attention than others. Some referees decide that they don't need a mentor, whilst others use theirs frequently - there are no hard-and-fast rules, and mentoring is not obligatory.

The best mentors offer a sympathetic ear and give clear and practical guidance. They are trusted and treat all their relationships with confidentiality unless otherwise instructed. Where it is obvious that one of their referees needs help, they may come to a game to watch that referee or, with the referee's permission, send an Adviser. Their full value can only be realised if referees contribute to the relationship and listen to the advice the mentor gives them.

Effectively, the mentoring system gives referees access to the Society's pool of experience and knowledge through an informal medium, allowing referees to discuss their aspirations, problems and concerns with a wise and trusted counsel.

Society friends/Club Advisers

As a further method of monitoring referee performance, some Societies have built a network of 'friends', people who will help the Society whenever they can and whose judgement is trusted and valued. Usually these friends are involved in the game as club coaches or administrators, and they will be standing on the touch-line during the game.

These people can give invaluable feedback to the Referee Society on the performance of their referees. They do not need to be trained Advisers, but they will still have an empathy for the game and they will instinctively know whether the referee is doing a good job and how he relates to the players. It's always useful to have another informed opinion on how a referee manages a game, especially when that opinion comes from someone who is not necessarily directly involved in refereeing. Their feedback and input can form another element in building an understanding of how referees perform, and many Societies are developing these contacts to add a further layer to their measurement and assessment routines.

The RFU has published a booklet, 'The Club Advisers Scheme', which provides more details for clubs and potential Advisers; this can be obtained from your local Referee Society.

What next?

Having got this far, you find yourself still interested in becoming a referee. You don't yet know whether you'll be any good, but no-one does - it's only when you get out there with a whistle in your hand that you'll discover that! But what do you have to do now to get started?

You could conceivably begin by jumping in at the deep end and refereeing some games at your local club. If you can get your hands on a current Law book, and you've had experience as a player, this is a possibility. However, many people nowadays prefer to do some basic referee training before they start: not only does this give you more confidence, but it also strengthens your position with regard to player safety and gives you the benefit of access to the Society's expertise and advice.

You will join the Society which covers the region in which you live. In some areas these Societies are grouped together with one Senior Society and a number of Associate Societies. In this case you would join an Associate Society and, if and when appropriate, you would move up to the Senior Society. Most Societies operate on a regional basis, so that you would not be expected to travel the length and breadth of the county or district each Saturday. However, the more senior you become, the more travelling will be expected of you, and you will find yourself on referee exchanges where you go to a completely different area under the control of another Society.

All the Referee Societies are listed in the Law book and the RFU Handbook (and a list of contacts is included in Appendix 2 on pages 117 to 120). You can also find out about the Societies by getting in touch with the RFU's Referee Department, and your local rugby club should have up-to-date details of whom to call. A lot of Societies have a dedicated Recruitment Secretary who will give you all the information and encouragement you need.

One of the first questions you will be asked by a Society is about your availability: 'When do you want to start?'. Whatever you decide to do, you should not be put under any pressure to start until you are happy to do so. No-one wants to send out a referee who isn't fully prepared, as that is the quickest way to damage the referee's confidence - and the players won't be happy, either. If you'd prefer to attend a Society meeting first, or go on a course or the Foundation Programme, make this clear and it will be noted and understood. As far as is possible, the Society will try and accommodate your requirements, but do bear in mind that it cannot expend unlimited amounts of energy on you if you never go near a game. Set yourself a target date to begin refereeing, and stick to it.

You should also remember to be pragmatic and realistic about your availability. Naturally your Society will want you to be available as much as possible, but they would much prefer to know that you are reliable for two Saturdays every month than unreliable for all of them. Do not over-promise or over-commit, as this will inevitably cause problems at some stage. You are not expected to be available all the time, but you are expected to be available when you say you will be.

Mutual expectations

As a referee and a member of a Society, you will have certain expectations, which might include the following.

- Fixtures will be arranged for you by the Society.
- Clubs will treat you with respect and good manners.
- You will be kept informed of changes in Law and interpretation.
- You will be offered training and development programmes.
- Your performance will be regularly monitored and assessed and you will receive objective and constructive feedback.
- You will be promoted solely on the basis of merit and potential.
- When you have concerns or questions, they will be given a proper hearing.
- You will be fully supported by your Society in matters concerning player discipline.

These are reasonable expectations and Societies try to live up to them. Equally, however, a Referee Society will expect certain things from you.

- You will keep the Society informed about your availability and will give as much notice as possible if this changes.
- You will inform the Society about relevant changes in personal circumstances (e.g. house move, change of contact details, injuries).
- You will act as an ambassador for refereeing in general and your Society in particular.
- You will always maintain the highest standards before, during and after your games.
- You will make every effort to encourage new recruits.
- You will keep yourself informed about developments in the game and will attend Society meetings and training sessions whenever possible.
- You will reach and maintain an appropriate level of fitness.
- You will, where possible, volunteer to help the Society's administration.

Becoming a referee demands these commitments, however frequently you turn out for your Society. You should bear in mind that the majority of Societies are entirely dependent on the income they earn from club subscriptions and therefore work to a very tight budget. If they spend money on phone calls and letters chasing recalcitrant referees, there will be less to spend on the more critical aspects of administration. Furthermore, a Society's administrators normally have full-time jobs and may well be active referees themselves, so their time is precious and limited: you can help them to use that time most effectively if you are co-operative and reliable. The Society is there to help you - but you must also help yourself and them.

And finally...

The game of rugby football is truly democratic. It accommodates all sizes and abilities - male and female - and every player can find their own level. The same applies to refereeing: regardless of your ambitions, the game will offer you a place in which you can enjoy yourself whilst significantly enhancing the enjoyment of players.

But, at whatever level you operate, you must never lose sight of the fundamental objective of the referee: **to manage an environment in which two sides can play and enjoy a game of rugby football within the Laws of the game**. You achieve this by applying the three basic principles of **safety, equity** and **the Laws**. Do this, and your contribution to the game will be respected and valued.

You won't always get it right, and you won't always be thanked even when you do. However, you will find that the more you learn, and the more you practice, the greater will be your enjoyment. The referee is the 31st player on the field, and his afternoon is just as important as the other 30 players. If players don't train, and don't work at their skills, they will not get as much out of the game as they might, and exactly the same is true for referees. Picking up the whistle doesn't mean that you stop the process of training, development and improvement; it simply means that you transfer your efforts to a different, and in many ways more challenging, discipline.

But, as a referee, you are still part of the game. One of the great strengths of rugby football is that the vast majority of referees are ex-players who have an enduring empathy with the game and all its participants. Becoming a referee does not automatically excommunicate you from that constituency. There is no 'us' and 'them' mentality in rugby and, as a referee, you are still considered to be a key participant.

There is no doubt that refereeing can be a stressful and challenging occupation, but it is, like any other skill, one that can be mastered through hard work, application, preparation and plenty of physical and mental training. You will only know how rewarding it can be when you've had a good game and both skippers want to buy you a drink afterwards.

More than ever, today's game needs good, qualified referees at all levels. This manual should be used as an aide-memoir, to remind you of what's involved and what's required, and is intended to form the basis of your preparation. But there is no substitute for going out on to the pitch and trying it for yourself - in exactly the same way as every other referee, be they at international or 'Extra B' level, began their careers. One final thought to carry with you on to the field of play: no-one succeeds as a rugby referee unless they enjoy it. It's a useful thing to bear in mind as you're running backwards in freezing January rain trying to remember the intricacies of the offside Law!

Recruitment FREEPHONE Number

For anyone interested in refereeing, a FREEPHONE telephone number has been set up by the RFU's Referee Centre of Excellence. For details of your local recruitment officer, call FREEPHONE **0800 834551.**

APPENDIX 1

Referee signals

Referee signals are recommended to aid communication between referees, players and spectators.

The signals have been divided into primary, secondary and tertiary categories.

Primary signals relate to decisions given by the referee (e.g. a try or a penalty) and their adoption by every referee is strongly recommended.

Secondary signals offer further clarification of a decision, and usually relate to and accompany a primary signal. Whilst each referee is encouraged to adopt the secondary signals shown, this is not compulsory.

Tertiary signals do not necessarily relate to any primary signals but are purely to assist the overall communication of the referee. Tertiary signals are employed entirely at the discretion of each individual referee.

With thanks to the following for appearing in the photographs: Brian Campsall, Nick Cousins, Steve Lander, Stewart Piercy, Ashley Rowden, Tony Spreadbury, Jerry Wallis, Chris White.

Primary signal - penalty kick

Arm fully extended at an angle of 60° to the horizontal, pointing in the direction of the non-offending side. Referee's shoulders parallel with touch-line.

Primary signal - free kick

Forearm raised vertically, upper arm horizontal. The arm should be pointing in the direction of the non-offending side. Referee's shoulders parallel with the touch-line.

Primary signal - try and penalty try

Arm fully extended vertically, pointing parallel to the touch-line; back parallel to the goal-line.

Primary signal - advantage

One arm outstretched at waist height in direction of non-offending side.

**Primary signal -
award of a scrummage**
Back parallel to the touch-line,
forearm horizontal pointing
to the side to put in the ball.

**Secondary signal -
forward pass/
throw forward**
Passing gesture with both hands
in front of body at waist height.

**Secondary signal -
knock on**
One hand above head,
tapped by other hand.

**Secondary signal -
not releasing ball
immediately**
Both arms to chest as if
holding the ball.

**Secondary signal -
wilfully falling over
or on a player**

Arched diving over gesture with
one arm in direction in which
offending player has fallen.
Signal given at chest height.

**Secondary signal -
diving to ground
in close proximity
of tackle**

Diving gesture with arm
from shoulder to waist height.

**Secondary signal -
pulling down**

Fist clenched, arm bent,
making pulling down
movement.

**Secondary signal -
pulling on**

Fist clenched, arm straight,
describing pulling on
movement, at shoulder
height.

**Secondary signal -
wheeling more than 90°**
Rotating index finger above
head, pointing downwards.

Secondary signal - foot-up
Raised heel and touch with
corresponding hand.

**Secondary signal -
put-in not straight**
Two hands slightly below waist
level describing passage of ball.

**Secondary signal -
improper binding**
One arm outstretched in a binding position, other hand moving
up outstretched arm as if to indicate the extent of a full bind.

Secondary signal - wilfully collapsing ruck or maul

Arms outstretched at shoulder height as if bound around an opponent. Modest lowering and twisting movement of upper body as if pulling opponent down on top of oneself.

Secondary signal - handling on ground in ruck or scrum

Sweeping movement of hand at ground level.

Secondary signal - not straight at line-out

Movement of hand, well above head, describing the path of the ball.

Secondary signal - closing gaps at line-out

Both hands (palms facing each other), fingers pointing upwards, accompanied by a squeezing movement of hands, at eye level.

Secondary signal - barging in line-out

Arms bent, barging movement of shoulder and arm away from body.

Secondary signal - leaning on line-out

Downward gesture with arm from shoulder height, palm of hand downward, arm slightly bent.

Secondary signal - pushing in line-out

Pushing gesture with both hands at shoulder height, palms vertical.

Secondary signal - lifting in line-out

Lifting gesture with both fists from waist to shoulder height.

Secondary signal - obstruction in general play

Both arms bent at elbow in front of chest, forearms at 90° to each other and palms facing referee.

Secondary signal - offside at line-out

Movement of hands and arm horizontally across chest in direction of offence.

Secondary signal - offside at ruck or maul (fringing)

Bent arm above head with hands describing a circle, fingers pointing downwards.

Secondary signal - offside at ruck, maul or scrummage (back foot)

Straight arm vertically downwards swinging in a vertical arc parallel to the offside line.

Secondary signal - offside (penalty or scrum back)
One arm as for a penalty kick, other arm indicating where kick taken and position of offside player. After alternative is selected, normal penalty kick or scrummage signal adopted.

Secondary signal - foul play (high tackle)
Movement of horizontal hand across front of neck.

Secondary signal - offside (remaining within 10m)
Rotating one hand in large circle above head.

Secondary signal - foul play (use of boot)

Stamping or other gesture with foot which mirrors the offence.

Secondary signal - foul play (punching)

One open hand above head punched by open fist.

Secondary signal - offside at ruck, maul or scrummage (back foot)

Straight arm vertically downwards swinging in a vertical arc parallel to the offside line.

**Tertiary signal -
formation of scrummage**
Both hands touching
above head, arms bent.

**Tertiary signal -
award of a 22m drop-out**
Arm outstretched horizontally
pointing towards centre
of 22m line.

**Tertiary signal -
'stay on your feet'**
Upward movement of both
hands, palms upwards, from
waist height.

APPENDIX 2

Referee Societies

Societies are listed by the following groups.

- **Combined Services Group of Rugby Union Referee Societies**
(Includes: Army, Royal Air Force, Royal Navy.)
- **Midland Group of Rugby Union Referee Societies**
(Includes: East Midlands, Leicestershire, North Midlands, Notts., Lincs. & Derby, Staffordshire, Warwickshire.)
- **Northern Counties Group of Rugby Union Referee Societies**
(Includes: Cumbria, Durham, Furness & District, Liverpool & District, Manchester & District, Northumberland, Yorkshire.)
- **South East Group of Rugby Union Referee Societies**
(Includes: Eastern Counties, Cambridge University & District, Essex, Norfolk, Suffolk & North Essex, Hampshire, Hertfordshire, Kent, London, Harrow & District, Metropolitan Surrey, South East London, Staines, Sussex.)
- **South West Group of Rugby Union Referee Societies**
(Includes: Berkshire, Buckinghamshire, Cornwall, Devon, Plymouth, Dorset & Wilts, Gloucester/Bristol, Gloucester & District, Oxfordshire, Somerset.)

COMBINED SERVICES GROUP

Referee Society Administrators
Army *Honorary Secretary*: Major D J Chapman RLC, Support Wing, HQ BVD, Ashchurch, Tewkesbury, Glos. GL20 8LZ (0115 9464414 (H) 01869 258301 (B) and 01869 258303 (Fax)). **Royal Air Force** *Honorary Secretary*: Wg Cdr I M Martin, 7 Park Lane, Brampton, Huntingdon PE18 8QD (01480 412921 (H)). *Training Officer*: Flt Lt J Burke, 4 Beacon Close, Stukley Meadows, Huntingdon, Cambs PE18 6GB (01480 431491 (H) 01480 52151 Ext 6864 (B) and 01480 52151 Ext 6850 (Fax)). **Royal Navy** *Honorary Secretary*: G Ashton Jones, 11 Buchan Avenue, Whiteley, Fareham, Hants, PO15 7EU (TBA (H) 01962 887714 (B) 01962 887643 (Fax) 0585 144847 (M)). *Training Officer*: A S Gribbon, 10 Hoylecroft Close, Fareham, Hants PO15 6BT (01329 236877 (H) and 01329 332350 (B) and 01329 332689 (Fax)).

MIDLAND GROUP

Divisional Referee Development Officer C. R. D. Leeke, Referee Centre of Excellence, Castlecroft Road, Wolverhampton. WV3 8NA (01604 24827 (B & F) and 0402 626266 (M)).

Referee Society Administrators
East Midlands *Honorary General Secretary*: C J Wright, 31 Fairmead Rise, Welford Road, Northampton NN2 8PP (01604 844766 (H) and 01604 844766 (Fax)). *Training & Development Officer:* J Burke, 4 Beacon Close, Stukeley Meadows, Huntingdon, Cambs, PE18 6GB (01480 431491 (H) 01480 52151 Ext 6866 (B)).

Leicestershire *Honorary Secretary*: I M Roberts, 16 Chapel Close, Houghton-on-the-Hill, Leicestershire LE7 9HT (0116 243 2228 (H) 01535 662551 (B) and 0116 243 3753 (Fax)). R *Training Officer*: M Mortimer, 34 Warwick Road, Littlethorpe, Leicestershire, LE9 5JA (0116 286 6201 (H & B)). *Training Officer*: R Sharp, 2 Duffield Avenue, Wigston, Leicester LE8 1FS (0116 288 2680 (H)). **North Midlands** *Honorary Secretary*: J Burgum, 19 Claines Road, Northfield, Birmingham B31 2EE (0121 475 6702 (H & Fax)). *Training Organiser*: N Sharpe, 270 Malvern Road, Worcester WR2 4PA (01905 423317 (H)). *Training Officer*: P Morgan, 58 Runnymede Road, Hall Green, Birmingham, B11 3BW (0121 608 6557 (H)). **Notts., Lincs. & Derby** *Honorary Secretary*: M R Yates, "Farthing's Cottage", Turner St, Kirton in Lindsey, Gainsborough, Lincolnshire DN21 4DB (0165 264 8084 (H) 0172 486 0151 (B) and 0172 427 1007 (Fax)). *Training Officer*: S J Bradford, 9 Elm Avenue, Long Eaton, Nottingham, Nottinghamshire NG10 4LR (0115 973 3533 (H) 0115 924 9924 Ext 43103 (B) and 0115 970 9944 (Fax)). **Staffordshire** *Honorary Secretary*: S C Lister, Ireland's Mansion, High Street, Shrewsbury, Shropshire SY1 1SQ (01743 271443 (H) 01743 231491 (B) and 01743 242275 (Fax)). *Training Officer*: I Hunter, 21 Severn Way Cressage, Shrewsbury, Shropshire, SY5 6DS (01952 510818 (H) 01743 235051 (W)). **Warwickshire** *Honorary Secretary*: S L Latham, 20 Heather Drive, Bedworth, Warwickshire CV12 0AT (01203 317775 (H & Fax)). *Development.& Training*: K Mahon, 3 Duncan Drive, Rugby, Warwickshire CV22 7RS (01788 810143 (H)).

NORTHERN GROUP

Divisional Referee Development Officer K. Bracewell, Referee Centre of Excellence, Castlecroft Road, Wolverhampton. WV3 8NA (01757 270412 (B & F)).

Referee Society Administrators

Cumbria *Secretary & Training Co-ordinator Senior*: A Jenkinson, 18 Station Road, Workington, Cumbria CA14 2JZ (01900 68960 (H) and 01946 825154 (B)). *Training Co-ordinator Junior*: M Strutt, Thirlmere House, 29 Strange Street, Keswick (017687 72697 (H)). *Training Officer*: G Matthews, 3 Frenchfield Way, Penrith, Cumbria CA11 8TW (01768 864992 (H) and 01900 65938 (B)). **Durham** *Secretary*: K P Eldridge, 18 Briar Walk, Darlington, Co Durham DL3 8QU (01325 465715 (H)). *Training Officer*: M J Lyons, 1 Warwick Drive, East Herrington, Sunderland SR3 3PU (0191 520 3198 (H) and 0191 386 5715 (B)). **Furness & District** *Honorary Secretary*: R. N. Rimmer, Langrigge Close, Langrigg Drive, Bowness on Windermere. LA23 3AF (01539 445540 (H) and 01539 720028 (B)). *Training Officer*: G Griffiths, The Police Station, Silecroft, Millom, Cumbria LA18 5LP (01229 772636 (H)). *Training Officer*: R N Rimmer, as above **Liverpool & District** *Honorary Secretary*: D A Yorke, 1a Sandown Terrace, Boughton, Chester CH3 5BN (01244 344026 (H) 0161 200 3463 (B) and 0161 200 3505 (Fax)). *Honorary Secretary* (I.O.M.): P Snellgrove, 5 Terence Avenue, Douglas, I.O.M. IM2 5BL (01624 662001 (H) and 01624 843181 (B)). *Training Officer*: R Wilkinson, Flat 7, Montagu Mews, Montagu Road, Freshfield, Formby, Merseyside L37 1LA (01704 832422 (H) and 01695 572625 (B)). **Manchester & District** *Honorary Secretary*: A Farmer, 22 Woodlands Park, Whalley, Clitheroe, Lancs, BB7 9UG (01254 824042 (H & Fax) 0973 305882 (Mobile). *Training Officer*: G Cove, 18 Princes Road, Sale, Cheshire, M33 3FF (0161 969 4253 (H)). **Northumberland** *Honorary Secretary*: D Barrow, 11 Hascombe Close, Beaumont Park, Whitley Bay, Tyne & Wear NE25 9XQ (0191 253 2072 (H)). *Training Officer*: A Beecroft, 120 Kingsway, Blyth, Northumberland NE24 2RX (01670 360444 (H) and 0191 268 2002 Ext 136 (B)). *Training Officer*: M Chestney, 54 Ventor Gardens, Low Fell, Gateshead NE9 6EA (0191 420 6947 (H)). **Yorkshire** *Honorary Secretary*: J L Lister, Park House, Akeds Road, Halifax HX1 2JG (01422 369255 (H) 01422 363498 (B) and 01422 321071 (Fax)). **North Yorks & Cleveland** *Secretary.*: M B Halliday, 30 Hunters Way, Dringhouses, York YO2 2JJ (01904 704493 (H)). **South Yorkshire** *Secretary:* A G MacGregor, 71 Ellers Avenue, Bessacarr, Doncaster DN4 7DZ (01302 538584 (H) 01302 382305 (B) and 01302 382254 (Fax)). **Central Yorkshire** *Secretary*: M Wells, 24 Netherdale Court, Wetherby LS22 6SW (01937 582114 (H) and 0113 2325235 (B)). **East Yorkshire** *Secretary*: M T

Tarran, 33 Northfield Close, South Cave, Brough HU15 2EW (01430 423557 (H)). **West Yorkshire** *Secretary:* G Dawkins, 13 Marriners Drive, Heaton, Bradford BD9 4JT (01274 496695 (H)). *Training & Development Officer:* Bracewell, Gleneige, West Lane, Burn, Selby, N. Yorkshire YO8 8LR (01757 270412 (H) and 01757 707731 (B)).

SOUTH EAST GROUP

Divisional Referee Development Officer D. Broadwell, Referee Centre of Excellence, Castlecroft Road, Wolverhampton. WV3 8NA (0181 777 4570 (B & F) 0802 435745 (M)).

Referee Society Administrators

Eastern Counties *General Secretary:* G Cross, Manor Farm, Roydon, Diss IP22 3QS (01379 642345 (H) 01379 640016 (Fax) and 0850 932903 (Mobile)). *Training & Development Sub-Committee Chairman:* P Storey, 26 The Green, Mendlesham Green, Stowmarket, Suffolk. IP14 5RQ (01449 767136 (H) 01473 296055 (B)). *Referee Development Officer:* M J Runswick, 3 Thrifts Walk, Chesterton, Cambridge CB4 1NR (01223 356239 (H) and 01223 402238 (B)). **Cambridge University & District** *General Manager:* M J Dimambro, 1 Coles Road, Milton, Cambridge CB4 6BL (01223 860972 (H and Fax)). *Training & Development Manager:* F Whaley, 125A Long Road, Cambridge CB2 2HE (01223 845310 (H)). *Training Officer:* T M Daniel, The New Barn, High Ditch Road, Fen Ditton, Cambridge CB5 8TF (01223 294317 (H)). **Essex** *Secretary:* E McLaughlan, 17 Halsham Crescent, Barking, Essex IG11 9HG (0181 594 4576 (H)). *Training Officer:* B Damer, 58 Spenser Road, Rainham, Essex RM13 8HB (01708 555734 (H)). *Training and Fitness:* D Locke, 17b Alderfords Street, Sible Hedingham, Nr Halstead, Essex CO9 3HX (01787 462510 (H)). **Norfolk** *General Secretary:* G Cross, Manor Farm, Roydon, Diss IP22 3QS (01379 642345 (H) 01379 640016 (B and Fax) and 0850 932903 (Mobile)). *Training Officer:* M. Salter, 51 Cromes Place, Coltishall. NR10 5JU (01603 736393 (H)). *Training Officer:* M. Brown, 47 Hillcrest Avenue, Toftwood Dereham. NR19 1LP (01362 698588 (H) 01362 697931 (B)). **Suffolk & North Essex** *Honorary. Secretary:* I Stewart, 7 Minster Road, Haverhill, Suffolk, CB9 0DR (01440 706076 (H) 01279 442611 (B)). *Training Officer:* P Storey, 26 The Green, Mendlesham Green, Stowmarket, Suffolk, IP14 5RQ (01449 767136 (H)). *Training Officer:* J Nicholson, 186 Defoe Road, Ipswich, Suffolk IP1 6RP (01473 743177 (H)). **Hampshire** *Administrator:* P Westley, 5 South Normandy, Warblington Street, Old Portsmouth, PO1 2ES, (01705 828794 (H)). *Secretary of Rugby:* T Mortimore, 555 Abbey Road, Basingstoke, Hampshire, RG24 9ER (01256 415775 (H)). *Training & Development Officer:* J Edwards, 10 Kennedy Crescent, Gosport, Hampshire, PO12 2NN (01705 589731 (H)). *Training Officer:* C Powell, 19 Pytchley Close, Hillhead, Fareham, Hants, PO14 3SF (01329 664145 (H)). **Hertfordshire** *Honorary Secretary:* P Freestone, 143 Wisden Road, Stevenage, Herts SG1 5NN (01438 721157 (H & Fax) 01923 260211 (B) and 0973 613422 (Mobile)). *Training Secretary:* E Bawden, 13 Hampton Close, Stevenage, Herts SG2 8SP (01438 811625 (H)). *Training Officer:* K Hurley, 139 Gordon Hill, Enfield, Middlesex EN2 0QT (0181 482 7992 (H)). **Kent** *Honorary Secretary:* T P Fagg, Hollis Barn Egerton, Ashford, Kent TN27 9BD (01233 756333 (H) 01233 624545 (B) and 01233 610011 (Fax)). *Training Officer:* C Booth, 4 Purcell Avenue, Tonbridge, Kent TN10 4DP (01732 356521 (H)). **London** *General Secretary:* E T H Evans, 7 Briar Walk, Putney, London SW15 6UD (0181 789 1347 (H) 0171 832 7047 (B) and 0171 832 7589 (Fax)). *Recruitment Secretary:* R W Ockenden, 19 Highbury Close, New Malden, Surrey KT3 5BY (0181 949 4420 (H)). *Training. & Development:* N D Cousins, The Orchard, Dulwich Common, London SE21 7EW (0181 693 3186 (H)). *Training Officer* (Surrey & Met. Kent): D J Turner, 49 Chelsham Road, Clapham, London SW4 6NN (0171 627 4778 (H) and 0171 926 9449 (B)). *Training Officer* (Middlesex): J Porter-Griffiths, 143b Swakeleys Road, Ickenham, Middlesex UB10 8DL (01895 637364 (H)). **Harrow & District** *Secretary:* R W G Wynde, 39 Shooters Avenue, Kenton, Middx HA3 9BQ (0181 907 7094 (H)). **Metropolitan Surrey** *Honorary Secretary:* R Greensted, 57 Canbury Park Road, Kingston Upon Thames, Surrey KT3 4SW (0181 549 4244 (H) and 0181 546 0272 (B)). *Training Secretary:* B Podmore, 18 Graham Road, Mitcham, Surrey CR4 2HA (0181 640 1520 (H)). **South East**

London *Honorary Secretary*: A A Stones, 46 Wellington Road, Bromley, Kent BR2 9NQ (0181 464 2083 (H) and 0171 387 7050 ext 4629 (B)). *Training Officer*: D J Turner, 49 Chelsham Road, Clapham, London SW4 6NN (0171 627 4778 (H) and 0171 926 9449 (B)). **Staines** *Referee Training*: B Wildin, 15 Douai Grove, Hampton, Middx TW12 2SR (0181 979 6817 (H)). **Sussex** *Honorary Secretary*: M P Madden, 4 Park Road, Burgess Hill, West Sussex, RH15 8ET (01444 245295 (H) 0171 600 6868 (B)). *Training Officer*: G Burtenshaw, "The Blenheims", Keymer Road, Burgess Hill, RH15 0BA (01444 232938 (H) and 0189 251 5350 (B)). *Recruitment Officer*: B G Griffiths, 6 Ravenswood, Hassocks, West Sussex BN6 8JB (01273 846028 (H)).

SOUTH WEST GROUP

Divisional Referee Development Officer W. A. Melrose, Referee Centre of Excellence, Castlecroft Road, Wolverhampton. WV3 8NA 01242 236999 (B & F).

Referee Society Administrators

Berkshire *Honorary Secretary*: P Emerson, 16 St Mary's Close, Henley-on-Thames, Oxfordshire RG9 1RD (01491 578606 (H) and 01734 401526 (B & Fax)). *Training Officer*: M Cock, 6 The Baxendales, Greenham, Berkshire RG14 7SA (01635 45508 (H)). **Buckinghamshire** *Honorary Secretary*: P Downes, Coxboro Dell, High Road, Cookham, Berks, SL6 9HR (01628 524881 (H) 0181 788 7272 (B)). *Fitness Officer*: T McDaid, 17 Otters Brook, Buckingham, Bucks MK18 7EB (01280 817491 (H)). *Training Officer*: A Randall, 55 Knaves Hill, Linslade, Leighton Buzzard, Beds. (01525 374034 (H)). **Cornwall** *Honorary Secretary*: J G Grindle, 1 Polwhele Road, Newquay, Cornwall TR7 2SJ (01637 874540 (H and Fax) and 0860 709728 (Mobile)). *Training Officer*: S A Hosking, 18 Codiford Crescent, Camborne, Cornwall TR14 8UF (01209 715073 (H)). **Devon** *Secretary*: R Gash, 59 Berkshire Drive, Exeter EX4 1NG (01392 270932 (H)). *Training Secretary*: K Beaumont, Pelistry, Rock Hill, Aveton Gillford, Kingsbridge, TQ7 4JT (01548 550166 (H)). **Plymouth** *Honorary Secretary*: J R Scott, 11 Tuxton Close, Plympton, Plymouth PL7 1QH (01752 330840 (H & Fax) 01392 201600 (B) and 01392 469860 (Fax)). *Training Officer*: N Higginson, 34 Goswella Gardens, Plymstock, Plymouth, PL9 9JG (01752 405877 (H)). **Dorset & Wilts** *Secretary*: A F Avery, 24 Wetherby Close, Milborne St Andrew, Blandford, Dorset DT11 0JN (01258 837450 (H)). *Training Officer*: I K Forward, Snowdon House, Gold Street, Stalbridge, Sturminster Newton, Dorset, DT10 2LX (01963 362540 (H)). *Recruitment Officer*: G Allsopp, 15 Guest Avenue, Branksome, Poole, Dorset, BH12 1JA (01202 733908 (H) 01202 715999 (B)). **Gloucester/Bristol** *Honorary Secretary*: R Bowie, 167 Bishop Road, Bishopston, Bristol BS7 8NA (0117 942 4332 (H)). *Training Officer*: G Weatherhead, 48 Beach Avenue, Severn Beach, Bristol BS12 3PB (01454 632225 (H)). **Gloucester & District** *Secretary*: G A Williams, 14 Greenhill Drive, Malvern, Worcs WR14 2BW (01684 563438 (H), 0976 819224 (M)). **Oxfordshire** *Honorary Secretary*: B Tomlin, 12 Mill Lane, Croughton, Brackley, Northants NN13 5LU (01869 810124 (H) (01869 810968 (Fax)). *Coaching and Training Officer*: A Davies, 6 Culham Close, Abingdon, OX14 2AS (01235 533568 (H)). **Somerset** *Honorary General Secretary:* G King, 13 Staddlestones, Midsomer Norton, Bath, BA3 2PP (01761 417 827 (H) 01761 413 869 (B) 01761 419348 (Fax)). *Training Officer*: T Starling, 28 Avon Close, Taunton, Somerset TA1 4SU (01823 337 877 (H)). *Fitness Officer*: R Simon, Watersmeet, Swingbridge, Bathpool, Taunton TA2 8BY (01823 286803 (H)). *Training Officer*: B Tinton, Sheraton, Back Lane, Draycott, Somerset, BS27 3TS (01934 743 039 (H)).